# Looking Back at
# Independent Double-Deckers
by
# Andrew Wiltshire

W T Edwards commenced trading around 1929 and initially operated lightweight coaches. Fords were the lightweight coaches of choice from the mid-1960s. Around fifty double-deckers were operated over the years, including several Leylands from Red & White and Ribble, though the last purchased were four Bristol FLFs from Bristol Omnibus in late 1977. Five AEC Regent Vs were operated between 1972 and 1978 and included 196-9 KFC, four out of a batch of five with low-bridge East Lancs bodies, the last low-bridge buses built for City of Oxford Motor Services. The fifth Regent V was 461 KTG, a thirty-foot forward-entrance model with Metro-Cammell bodywork, and one of twenty new to Rhondda Transport in 1961. It passed to Western Welsh in

1971, and was sold to Edwards in 1973. 461 KTG is noted at Joys Green on 11 April 1975 receiving attention from a mechanic. Edwards was for many years, with around forty vehicles, the largest operator in the Forest, mainly due to contracts providing staff transport to the large Rank Xerox factory at Mitcheldean. Edwards became part of the Birmingham-based Paul Tizard Group in 1973, following which, the livery changed from green to dark blue. In 1982, the Joys Green operation was sold, along with around a dozen vehicles, to a new operator, Dean Forest Coaches Ltd, and Edwards concentrated on a much smaller operation at their Gloucester depot, which only lasted until 1983.

*(John Wiltshire)*

# INTRODUCTION

I have for many years had an interest in the traditional independent fleets that operated around the UK, and in particular, those that ran double-deckers. This is a big subject to cover in one book, but I have tried to include a broad representation of operators, large and small, well known and more obscure, as well as a good variety of vehicle types.

Some fleets that I have covered were stage-carriage operators from the outset, and often invested in new vehicles on a regular basis. Others made their living from contract work, relying on decent used double-deckers being available at a reasonable price. I have also taken the opportunity to include some double-deck buses that have adopted a more unusual role with a private owner.

The period covered in this volume extends from the 1960s and through the 1970s to a cut-off point around 1985. The early years of deregulation have been deliberately avoided as they deserve a separate volume. I am sure most readers will find plenty of interest, and hopefully this book will bring back some happy memories of what is now in most cases just history.

## Acknowledgements

A very large thank you must go to John Jones and Cliff Essex for their photographic contributions and for the time and effort put into researching matters relating to this project. I am also very grateful to Pete Brabham for taking time and great care to scan and tidy up a number of the images that I have selected. Bernard McCall has once again given his enthusiastic support and backing for this latest volume, while my wife Tracey has given her encouragement while I spend time researching and writing, having embarked on yet another project. As always, many thanks go out to all my colleagues from the Transport Museum at Wythall for their continued support and interest in my publications, and especially Malcolm Keeley for providing some rather splendid images.

Written sources of reference used include copies of Ian Allan British Bus Fleets, Buses magazines, Capital Transport and British Bus Publishing Bus Handbooks, PSV Circle fleet histories, numerous publications on operators' fleet histories and various Fleetbooks by A M Witton.

Andrew Wiltshire    Cardiff    September 2015

*Front cover:* For many years until the 1980s there were always a handful of small independent owners in Cornwall that kept a few double-deckers mainly for use on school contracts in their local area. E J Deeble and Son, based at The Garage in the village of Upton Cross near Liskeard, were a well-known and long established operator. They ran stage services to places like Liskeard, Looe and Polperro, as well as a fleet of coaches. From the 1960s they ran mainly saloons, but occasionally had a double-decker in their fleet. In 1975, Deeble was running this rather interesting and recently-acquired Leyland Atlantean, which was photographed near Polperro on 17 September. VAM 944 was originally one of the quartet of low-height Weymann-bodied Atlanteans, which were purchased new by Silver Star Motor Services Ltd of Porton Down, Wiltshire, between 1959 and 1962. In June 1963 Silver Star were taken over by Wilts and Dorset who had no use for the Atlanteans and they were sold. VAM 944 passed to Bristol Omnibus briefly before moving to Super of Upminster in 1964 and Berresford of Cheddleton in 1967. After just two years it was with Hale-Trent Cakes of Clevedon who ran it until 1975, when it passed to Deeble. Of special note is the ornate beading on the body, an extra touch specified by Silver Star. VAM 944 continued to serve Deeble until October 1978.

*(Malcolm Keeley)*

*Back cover:* Moving from Hilton to Fenstanton in 1977, Whippet Coaches purchased a handful of new double-deckers. These included a handsome Willowbrook-bodied Leyland Atlantean in 1966, and then in 1973 an impressive long-wheelbase Atlantean AN68 with a Northern Counties body that had seats for 83 passengers. During the 1960s Whippet had purchased small numbers of AEC Regent IIIs from London Transport of both RT and RLH variety. They returned to former London Transport vehicles again in 1983 when LT decided to dispose of its MCW Metropolitan MD class. These were modern-looking dual-door integral vehicles dating from 1976/77, and based on the Scania BR111DH running units. Over a ten year period Whippet acquired eighteen former London examples and at least eight of them were later rebuilt to single-door layout. One such example was KJD 271P seen here in Ramsey in June 1984. It was formerly London Transport MD71 and served with Whippet from 1984, later passing to Imperial of Rainham by 2000. Whippet moved to new premises at Swavesey in 2009 and, trading as Go Whippet, continued to buy used double-deckers from London. In November 2014 the business was taken over by Australian-owned Transit Systems.

*(John Wiltshire collection)*

Massey-bodied Daimler CVD6 DD1 (KAL578) belonging to W Gash and Sons Ltd of Newark is seen leaving Nottingham's Broad Marsh bus station on 5 April 1980, a truly remarkable survivor. William Gash bought a Beeston-Humber lorry in 1921 and converted it to carry passengers, but replaced it the following year with a Ford Model T. He would carry passengers from Elston into Newark, but was soon running into Nottingham. Following WWII, Gash purchased a number of new Daimler CVD6 chassis and had the first four completed with Strachan low-bridge bodies. They entered service as DD1-3 (KAL 578-80) in 1948 joined by DD4 (KNN 622) in 1949. Further examples followed as DD5-9, but received different bodies. Meanwhile Gash moved to smart new premises at Bowbridge

Road, Newark in May 1953 and became a limited company in 1954. By the late 1950s there were issues with the condition of the Strachan bodies on Daimlers DD1-4, and the bodies were scrapped. The chassis of DD2 to DD4 were then sent to Massey Bros to receive new 61-seat high-bridge layout bodies with platform doors. After a number of years in storage, DD1 followed in 1962. In later years DD1 tended to be confined mainly to local schools contracts, but was still in use with Gash in 1986. It later passed into preservation while sister bus DD2 (KAL 579) is also preserved at the Transport Museum, Wythall near Birmingham.

(John Jones)

Warstone Motors Ltd which traded as Green Bus Service was a relative newcomer to bus operations and should not be confused with the Green Bus Company of Rugeley, which passed to Midland Red in November 1973. Warstone Motors commenced in 1974, and was based at Great Wyrley near Cannock in Staffordshire. Their first vehicle was a 1950 Bedford OB and by 1982 a small network of services had been developed in the surrounding area. The company director Graham Martin specialised in using older vehicles that were always immaculately turned out in the fleet's two-tone green and cream livery carrying the Green Bus Service fleet name. Yellow was later added to the livery. The first double-decker owned was YTH 815, a 1962 Guy Arab IV with a low-bridge Massey body that came from Rees and Williams of Tycroes in 1977,

and is seen here at Cannock on 16 July 1977. It remained in the fleet until sold to the 447 Group of Pembrey for preservation. It became vandalised, but in 2010 was rescued by the Swansea Bus Museum and now awaits restoration. Saloons always formed the backbone of the Green Bus fleet, but in 1981 a Leyland PD3 again with a low-bridge Massey body was obtained from Rhymney Valley District Council, while later additions included PD3s of Bradford and Stockport origin. A number of other double-deckers were later added to the fleet including a Daimler Fleetline and quite a variety of Leyland Atlanteans. In later years there was a move from full-size saloons to minibuses. Operating difficulties forced the closure of the business in November 2009.

*(John Jones)*

Edmund Wright a former coal miner lived in Penycae, a village to the south-west of Wrexham. In 1924 he acquired a Ford Model T, and with assistance from his son Charles, put the vehicle to work carrying miners. Trading as Wright and Son, in between these duties, the Ford performed stage carriage work. Upon his death in 1952, Charles took over and traded as Wrights Coaches, while Charles' son Michael joined the business in 1959. A revolutionary three-year old Guy Wulfrunian double-decker was purchased in August 1964. LEN 101 had come from Howells and Withers of Pontllanfraith in South Wales, but had been new to Bury Corporation as their 101 in 1961 and had a Roe 73-seat body. The Wulfrunian was not a successful bus. On the positive side it offered a high seating capacity, a front entrance with a flat-floor and a reliable Gardner engine. Its major flaws were its air-suspension and all-round disc brakes. Bury could not wait to be rid of it, but Wrights persevered and ran the bus until January 1970, whereupon it was replaced by a new Seddon saloon. LEN 101 is seen shortly before passing to the well-known Staffordshire fleet, Berresfords of Cheddleton, who did not run the bus in service but laid it up. It was rescued for preservation in the 1980s, but was badly damaged by another bus whilst in storage in Manchester, and in 2015, just its chassis survives.

*(Cliff Essex)*

LCO 852 is a Leyland PD2/12 with a 56-seat Metro-Cammell body and dates from 1956. It was new to Plymouth City Transport as their 52 and was one of a batch of twenty-four, their first PD2s with non-Leyland bodywork, which had ceased to be available from 1954. LCO 852 is seen at the bus terminus on The Moor in Falmouth on 6 August 1974. It is now working for Grenville Motors Ltd of Camborne and still wears Plymouth livery. Grenville, based at Troon near Camborne, had begun trading in 1947, growing their business by acquiring small local operators, often with stage-carriage services, from the 1950s and into the 1970s. Single-deckers and coaches were the norm, but a number of double-deckers have been operated over the years including at least a dozen Leylands from Plymouth. These included Leyland PD1s obtained in 1960 and later a sister bus to LCO 852 in the shape of MCO 660. During the 1980s a number of ex Plymouth Atlanteans, were acquired for schools services, and could often be found garaged at the Penryn outstation. Grenville Motors was unable to continue trading profitably in the aftermath of deregulation, and was taken over by former NBC subsidiary Western National in March 1988.

*(John Wiltshire)*

The name Delaine is instantly associated with a fleet of exceptionally well turned out buses and coaches based upon the Lincolnshire village of Bourne, a reputation which has carried on for years and continues to be the case in 2015. The origins of this splendid operator can be traced back as far as 1890 when horse-drawn vehicles were used to transport people to local markets. Motor bus operation commenced in 1919 with a 14-seat Ford Model T running once a week to either Spalding, Stamford or Grantham. The main route was however to Peterborough introduced in 1923, and after becoming Delaine Coaches Ltd in 1941, the first double-deckers were introduced in 1948. Early examples were of Crossley manufacture followed by an AEC Regent III and later Leyland Titans of PD2 and PD3 variety. The two PD3s were unique as being the only double-deckers to be bodied by Yeates of Loughborough. In 1966 Delaine purchased this Leyland Atlantean 60 (DTL 489D) which was fitted with a 76-seat Willowbrook body, and served the fleet until 1983 and is now in private preservation. It is seen at Delaine's depot in July 1970. Used double-deckers were the policy from 1973 until 1995 when Delaine purchased the first of six new Volvo Olympians. Volvo has since been the sole choice for the double-deck fleet with no fewer than seventeen B7TL and B9TL models being purchased since 2000.

*(Cliff Essex)*

*Above:* Cornish operator Roselyn Coaches of Par can be traced back to the 1920s, and has been run by the Ede family for the last sixty years or so. By 1966 Roselyn was using double-deckers for school contract work in the area, and from the start, AECs were a popular choice, obtained from a number of sources. Six Regent Vs originally with Maidstone and District joined the Roselyn fleet between September 1971 and June 1973, and included this example VKR 470. New in 1956 it had a Park Royal body and is noted at the depot on 12 August 1974. The first to be sold was VKR 480 which passed to a South Wales operator in 1973, the last being VKR 470 which went to Smith, Gillingham in May 1980 for preservation. Other interesting AECs owned included at least five of the eleven forward-entrance Regent Vs that were new to the Atomic Energy Research Establishment (AERE) of Harwell in 1962. Eventually rear-engine double-deckers appeared, and during the 1980s and 1990s these included former Derby Fleetlines and Plymouth Atlanteans, plus a host of Bristol VRTs. In 2015 Roselyn operates around twenty five coaches as well as double-deckers, and they are still based at Middleway Garage on St Blazey Road in Par.

*(John Wiltshire)*

*Above right:* Based in the Forest of Dean, Frederick Cottrell began his motorbus operation in 1921. His first double-decker was a wartime utility Daimler CWA6 with a Brush body, delivered in 1944 and used extensively on the Gloucester service. New and used double-deckers continued to be added to the fleet and of note were a couple of all-Leyland Titans in 1947 and 1950. The first thirty-foot AEC Regent V built came to Cottrell's as SDF 281, replacing the utility Daimler in November 1956 and lasting until 1975, while a shorter forward-entrance version arrived in 1960, but was sold after just eight years. The Gloucester service remained in the hands of double-deckers throughout the 1970s, and the last new addition was EAD 122T in 1979. This was a long-wheelbase Leyland Fleetline with a Northern Counties body, and here it is seen passing through its picturesque home village of Mitcheldean, bound for Ruardean on 21 July 1981. All subsequent double-deck additions were used vehicles and included Metrobuses and a rare Leyland Lion. Cottrell's gave up the stage services in 2004, and the family closed down the business in 2007.

*(John Wiltshire)*

Charlton-on-Otmoor Services was a small independent operator founded in the 1920s, and hailed from the Oxfordshire village of that name. The business had a number of different proprietors in the early years, but by 1958 it was being run by G.P. Holder. Two former London Transport RT-type AEC Regents were owned for many years and used to transport military personnel to the many camps in the area north of Oxford. In this view we see AEC Regent V MCY 407 parked outside St. Mary the Virgin church opposite the operator's garage in Charlton-on-Otmoor on 28 February 1976. It is an early example of this model dating from 1955, and has a Weymann 59-seat body fitted with platform doors.

It was new to South Wales Transport, but obtained from Whippet of Hilton in 1968. A second former South Wales Transport Regent V YCY 804, was obtained in December 1975, but this was a thirty-foot model with Willowbrook bodywork and a forward-entrance. As for MCY 407, it was eventually purchased for preservation by some enthusiasts from South Wales in 1982, and initially restored and rallied. After many subsequent years in storage the bus is now under restoration at the Swansea Bus Museum, and is the oldest surviving AEC Regent V in existence.

*(John Jones)*

Located in Northumberland, Ashington was a major centre of the coal mining industry. Bedlington & District Luxury Coaches were based in the town, and it was their colliery contracts for which they will be remembered. They ran a fascinating collection of mainly double-deckers on a large number of miners' services throughout the south Northumberland coalfield. Their red and white buses included Bristol LS, KSW and LD models, numerous ex London Transport RTs plus AEC Regents including this former City of Oxford example WJO 185. It was a 1956 AEC Regent V with an exposed radiator and Park Royal low-bridge bodywork, and is seen in July 1971. An interesting selection of AEC Bridgemasters and Renowns was also owned at one stage as well as some unusual single-deck AEC Regent Vs from South Wales Transport. The livery eventually changed to green and cream, and the fleet continued to acquire large numbers of double-deckers. Latterly, former Nottingham AEC Renowns and Leyland Atlanteans were popular. The collapse of the mining industry brought about the end of Bedlington and District, which it is thought ceased around April 1994.

*(Cliff Essex)*

Premier (Harold Wilson Ltd) was one of the well-known Doncaster area independents and was based at East Lane, Stainforth, throughout its sixty-eight year existence. Harold Wilson commenced in 1924 and is thought to have been the pioneer operator on the service from Doncaster to Thorne running via Edenthorpe which was later run jointly with a number of other small independents. In 1940 the first double-decker was purchased, an ex Leeds Guy Arab and paved the way for the arrival of many more Guy Arabs to the Premier fleet. In the early post-war years three Arab IIIs were purchased new, one featuring a Barnaby body, while the Arab IV followed with the fourth one having a forward-entrance. In addition to stage service work, works contracts were an important source of revenue and a small coach fleet was also maintained. A new Daimler Fleetline arrived in 1965, the first example in the area and new double-deckers continued to be purchased in the 1970s. In 1976 Premier took delivery of an Alexander-bodied Volvo Ailsa B55, NET 520R, which we see here at the depot in April 1985. This front-engined double-decker was a most unusual purchase for an English independent operator and remained on fleet strength until 1988 when Harold Wilson's business was taken over. The fleet livery was originally dark blue and cream, but light blue and even a small amount of red featured as time went on.

*(Cliff Essex)*

Cheltenham has always been an interesting place for independent buses, and over the years a number of fleets were based there, while others have regularly worked into the town. Harry Leach (Harry's Mini Coach) commenced trading in 1963 and later became Harry's Coaches Ltd, based in Cheltenham. A number of former Portsmouth Leyland PD2 double-deckers were acquired in 1973 from Shropshire dealer Lionel Amos of Onibury, to cover some schools contracts. In January 1974 Lionel Amos acquired the assets of Harry's Coaches and set up Ladvale Ltd, based in Cheltenham. This new venture grew rapidly acquiring other operators in the area and within a few years had eighty vehicles. The Harry's Coaches fleet included PFR 342, an ex Blackpool Leyland PD2/27 with full-fronted Metro-Cammell Orion bodywork, and dated from 1959. It is in company with former Portsmouth ORV 990 in the depot yard at Cheltenham on 14 June 1975, and at this point Ladvale were down to just two double-deckers. PFR 342 was withdrawn in May 1978 and was reported out of use in the former Applegate's yard at Heathfield, Berkeley, by September that year. Ladvale closed down its Cheltenham base and eventually ceased operating altogether in 1984.

*(John Wiltshire)*

In 1926 J Stevenson began running a service from Uttoxeter to Beamhurst along the Cheadle road using a 16-seat Reo. The business rapidly expanded and by 1930 Stevenson was operating more routes with around eight buses. In 1941 a limited company was formed but the official title Stevenson's of Uttoxeter Ltd did not appear until 1972. In 1945 a Guy Arab utility was the first double-decker acquired and subsequently, used double-deckers have been a dominant feature of this fleet, but saloons and coaches were also purchased. The yellow and black Stevenson fleet, based at Spath just outside Uttoxeter, remained at around thirty vehicles from the post-war years until about 1972 and random fleet numbering continued to be used. The subject of this view taken at Burton-on-Trent bus station on 14 June 1973 is 27 (6349 WJ). This bus was a thirty-foot AEC Regent V with a 69-seat Roe body and was new to Sheffield Joint Omnibus Committee as 1349 in 1960. Amongst the half-cab double-deckers operated by Stevenson were a number of former London Transport RTLs, an RTW plus further AEC Regent Vs from City of Oxford and Devon General. Leyland Titans were also popular with PD2s from Brighton, Wigan and Burnley and Pendle and a pair of PD3s also from Sheffield. In 1981 a former Northern General forward-entrance AEC Routemaster was a novel addition to the fleet.

*(John Jones)*

Weardale Motor Services still operates in County Durham to the west and north-west of Bishop Auckland, with local services, school contracts and a very smart coach fleet, based in Stanhope and Frosterley. By 1926 a number of operators were involved running a service from Stanhope to Crook, and from 1930 Oliver Stanley Gibson had a 50% share of this. In 1955 Gibson acquired the business of Stanhope Motor Services together with a number of routes. This was kept as a subsidiary for a number of years but all vehicles wore red, maroon and white fleet colours. A handful of double-deckers were owned from the 1950s and included a Leyland Tiger in the Stanhope M S fleet that received a new Roe double-deck body in 1958, and a new Alexander-bodied Leyland PD3 for the main fleet, the following year. A few new saloons were purchased subsequently and in 1970 this splendid long-wheelbase Leyland Atlantean GUP 6H arrived. It had a 78-seat dual-door body by Roe and was basically built to a standard Leeds City Transport design. It was seen in Wolsingham on 1 December 1981 while engaged on school duties. By this time the double-deck fleet was much larger and consisted of many fine Leyland PD2 and PD3 double-deckers, all required for schools contracts. GUP 6H was the only rear engine vehicle for many years, and it eventually departed by 1995, along with the Titans, to be replaced by newer vehicles including Olympians.

*(Andrew Wiltshire)*

Lewington was an Essex-based independent operator, who during the 1970s had addresses at Cranham near Hornchurch and Harold Hill to the north east of Romford. It is thought that the business dated back to the mid-1960s trading as Lewington Hire Services, when a former West Yorkshire Bristol K5G was owned. Over the years they operated a large and somewhat varied fleet of buses and coaches most of which were engaged purely in contract work. A visit to their Harold Hill premises on 4 June 1977 produced this nice view of early Leyland Atlantean HHF 10, which was new to Wallasey Corporation (10) in March 1960. It had a Metro-Cammell body and initially passed via Merseyside PTE, then to Cambridgeshire independent Burwell and District in September 1974 where it

had a rather unhappy existence, before moving on to Lewingtons in late 1976. Also on site that day was a former Cardiff AEC Bridgemaster TUH 366 that had come from Whippet Coaches of Hilton. Lewington operated a number of other interesting double-deckers which included three open-top Guy Arab IIIs FFN 377/9/84, that were new to East Kent, at least three former Western SMT Daimler Fleetlines and two former City of Nottingham Fleetlines. As for saloons, here too there was much variety, but the AEC Reliance proved very popular. It is thought that around 1979 the fleet-name changed to Lewington (Bordabus) and that an address at Abridge was in use shortly after this date.

*(John Jones)*

With premises at George Elliot Street in Nuneaton, J Lloyd and Sons was founded in 1924. Nuneaton was a textile-manufacturing town located in the Warwickshire coalfield and close to the industrial city of Coventry, which resulted in Lloyds obtaining numerous works contracts in the area. For these services there was a requirement for double-deckers, and many interesting types were operated over the years. Well remembered by many were the eight ex London Transport AEC RT-type Regents, while perhaps the most interesting vehicle was former Leyland prototype Lowloader STF 90 which was a forerunner of the Atlantean. This Saunders-Roe-bodied double-decker joined the fleet in September 1958 and was sold in 1961. Four former Barton rebuilds with

Northern Counties full-fronted, low-bridge, forward-entrance bodywork were operated, the last of these bowing out as late as 1981. Our view is of VET 138, a bus which remained in the fleet until 1980 when it was sold for scrap. It was a 70-seat AEC/Park Royal Bridgemaster dating from 1961 that Lloyds acquired in February 1973. It was previously Rotherham Corporation 138, and one of five similar buses that this undertaking had purchased in 1961. All were withdrawn in the years 1971/72 and four saw further service. It was not until July 1994, when based at Avenue Road, Nuneaton, that Lloyds ceased to trade.

*(The Transport Museum Wythall collection)*

**Distinctive Liveries.** South Yorkshire Road Transport Limited (SYRT), of Pontefract, was formed in 1973 when it inherited the assets and services of South Yorkshire Motors Limited. It was at this time that this striking livery was introduced. Although coaches were operated, the mainstay of the operator's activities were the five major stage-carriage services, for which a fleet of double-deckers was maintained. Early double-deckers with South Yorkshire Motors Limited featured examples of Albion and Leyland manufacture, the last half-cab being a Leyland PD3 in 1960, all being of low-bridge layout. The first of a quartet of Leyland Atlanteans arrived in 1963 and were fitted with Weymann semi-lowbridge bodywork, as found in many BET fleets at this time. One of these was 85 (391 GWT) seen on 15 April 1983 at the Pontefract depot at Northgate. The bus is now near the end of its life and would be used increasingly on school contracts. Further Atlanteans were later added to stock, the Daimler Fleetline (with a Leyland 680 engine) and Northern Counties bodywork becoming the preferred model for SYRT from 1973. SYRT continued after deregulation, and was eventually bought out by the Caldaire Group in July 1994, by which time the standard double-decker had become the Leyland Olympian.

*(Andrew Wiltshire)*

Red Rover was for many years a household name in the bus industry as well as amongst enthusiasts. Its origins can be traced back to 1924 when Edward Cain started operating a Dennis double-decker in London on routes 14 and 49. Red Rover Omnibus Ltd was established in 1927 and a coach service from Aylesbury to London began the following year. In 1934 the London routes were taken over by the London Passenger Transport Board, and Red Rover made Aylesbury its new base with local services being introduced. The Dennis chassis was popular until 1951, and Daimlers and AECs were also operated, the latter becoming very popular until the 1970s. The business was acquired by coach operator Keith Garages in 1955, who continued to run the Red Rover fleet separately. Red Rover purchased no fewer than thirteen RT-type AEC Regents from London

Transport after 1956 supplemented by two RTLs and RTW124. KXW 314 was RT1668 when operating as a London bus and was new in 1950 with a Park Royal body, but had received the 1948 Weymann body originally fitted to RT479 by the time it was acquired in 1964. It is seen in Aylesbury working for Red Rover in August 1970. Three AEC double-deckers were bought new in the late 1950s and early 1960s, two Bridgemasters and a Renown, while further AEC double-deckers were obtained second-hand. A small number of saloons was always maintained as well as a fleet of coaches, and this continued to be the case after deregulation in 1986. Red Rover was taken over by Luton and District in 1987.

*(Cliff Essex)*

Arthur Mayne acquired his first purpose-built passenger vehicle in 1925, and from 1926 put it to work on a service from Audenshaw to the centre of Manchester. In June 1932 he was granted a licence to continue operating from Audenshaw to Manchester via the Ashton New Road, subject to certain conditions. Double-deck operation started in 1934 with a new AEC Regent and others followed, all of forward-entrance layout which was unusual at that time. Two very smart AEC Regent IIIs arrived in 1949, but used double-deckers were also added to stock between 1945 and 1956. From 1957 advantage was taken of the recently permitted length of thirty feet for double-deck vehicles, and that year saw the delivery of three AEC Regent Vs with attractive Park Royal bodies. Mayne returned for three more in 1961, but these had the rather angular style of Park Royal body. Two more but this time with East Lancs bodywork entered the fleet in 1964, while the final half-cabs for Mayne were CXJ 520-2C delivered in 1965 with similar bodies, but built in Sheffield by East Lancs' associated company Neepsend. Here we see CXJ 522C at the Manchester terminus at Stevenson Square. After deregulation in 1986, the Mayne business grew rapidly as new services were taken on, but sadly the service bus side of A Mayne and Son Ltd of Clayton was bought out by Stagecoach Manchester in January 2008. Mayne continues in 2015 purely as a coach operator.

*(Andrew Wiltshire collection)*

The Wood family began rearing poultry near Wistanstow, Shropshire, in 1881 and J P Wood & Sons later opened poultry shops in nearby Craven Arms as well as Ludlow and other local towns. During the 1950s and 1960s, J P Wood's sons took the poultry industry to a new level, by founding the giant poultry-producing business Chukie Chicken. This was based at The Grove, near Craven Arms and at its peak employed 1400 workers. A fleet of used coaches was maintained for staff transport and later examples of former London Transport RF, RFW and GS classes were operated. In 1969 Mr Ted Jones became transport manager, and buses began to be sourced from NBC subsidiaries. These included AEC Reliances from Maidstone and District, City of Oxford and West Riding. The Bristol/ECW combination was then favoured, and witnessed the arrival of a number of LS and MW saloons as well as a pair of early RELLs from Red and White. Some double-deckers were purchased for a number of runs and these included a pair of former Crosville Bristol FLF6Bs. One of these is JFM 243D new in 1966 as Crosville DFB243 and is seen at Craven Arms on 31 August 1981. When Chukie Chicken was bought out by Unilever, the smartly turned out blue and white buses disappeared from the Craven Arms area altogether. The Wood family then turned to brewing real ale.

*(John Wiltshire)*

PRIGG LANE

South Petherton is a large village in Somerset which was historically a market town. It is located about ten miles west of Yeovil and was surprisingly home to two well-known independent operators, Safeway Services and Hutchins and Cornelius. The latter came into being in 1934 following the amalgamation of two operators, Hutchings Omnibus Services of South Petherton and Cornelius Services of nearby Barrington. As the last of the proprietors retired in 1954, the business passed to Vincents, the Yeovil-based motor dealer. By the 1960s three main routes were operated taking Hutchins & Cornelius into the towns of Taunton, Yeovil and Crewkerne. Saloons and coaches formed the majority of the fleet, but in 1958 a new Dennis Loline was acquired for the Yeovil service. This was sold for export in 1973, its replacement being a smart ECW-bodied Bristol VRT. Registered RYA 700L, this bus was the first example of a VRT purchased by a UK independent, and is seen here entering South Petherton from Yeovil on 29 May 1975, having completed a day's work. The livery changed many times over the years but maroon and cream was adopted by the late 1960s. For commercial reasons, the business came to an abrupt end on 31 May 1979, with some services passing to neighbouring operator Safeway Services.

*(John Wiltshire)*

The Potteries area of Staffordshire was home to several small independent operators of stage-carriage services. William Stonier was one of the earliest of these and had commenced business at Hanley in 1915. By 1922 he was running three buses and moved to a new base at Goldenhill to the north of Tunstall. His main service for many years ran between Kidsgrove and Meir and the fleet remained confined to about five vehicles until just after WWII. The 1950s witnessed a rapid expansion in the Stonier business which now provided services to a new housing estate at Bentilee. From 1953 this was jointly operated with PMT, and Stonier used second-hand double-deckers. The preference was for Leylands and they ran numerous examples of PD1, PD2 and PD3 models obtained from many different sources. Number 8 (909 EUM) was a 1963 Leyland PD3A/1 with Roe 73-seat bodywork and platform doors. It had originally operated for Farsley Omnibus Company Limited, Leeds, and was purchased by Stonier in 1972 from Wallace Arnold subsidiary Hardwick Services Limited. It is seen here in Hanley bus station on 24 April 1973. Stonier sold its business to Berresfords of Cheddleton in 1978 and it remained a separate fleet within the Berresford Group, later relocating to new premises in Tunstall. The Stonier name disappeared in 1987 when the Berresford Group sold out to the newly-privatised PMT.

*(John Jones)*

The Dennis Loline proved to be a popular double-decker on the second-hand market with its overall low height and reliable Gardner engine. The majority were to forward-entrance layout, including 399 COR, a former Aldershot and District Loline Mk III model, operated by W Norfolk & Sons of Nayland photographed at Colchester in July 1972. This bus had an Alexander body with seating for 68, and had been new in 1961 as Aldershot and District 399. It was acquired in January 1972, and, as their own livery was similar, Norfolk chose to leave the bus in its original colours. This very old family concern was based at Mill Street in the Suffolk village of Nayland, north of Colchester on the A134. The business can be traced back to the 1868, and they operated their first motor bus in 1918 and first double-decker in 1922. The main service was to Colchester, and until 1976 was jointly run with Eastern National, after which Norfolk ran it alone. Double-deckers were always in the minority, and until the 1980s; there was usually only one in the fleet at a time. After WWII, a number of AEC Regents were operated, and after the Dennis Loline departed in 1976, Norfolk purchased a selection of Daimler Fleetlines and later Bristol VRTs. The Norfolk business passed to Hedingham and District Omnibuses in April 1991, who retained the Norfolk identity for a short while.

*(John Wiltshire)*

One of the more interesting independents in the Midlands could be found working to the south of Nottingham. The distinctive dark blue, maroon and cream livery was for decades associated with buses of the South Notts Bus Co Ltd of Gotham. In 1928 Mr C T Dabell began operating his main route from Gotham running north to Nottingham, which was later extended southwards to Loughborough. Barton Transport later purchased a 50% share in South Notts, which continued to be run as a separate concern by the Dabell family. In 1951 double-deckers first appeared when South Notts began running to the new Clifton Estate to the south of Nottingham, jointly with Nottingham City Transport and West Bridgford Urban District Council. Initially, double-deckers would be to low-bridge layout and from the early 1950s, Leyland PD2s and later PD3s were acquired. The last two PD3s had forward-entrance low-bridge bodies like 76 (76 LNN) seen here at Loughborough. It was a PD3/6 model, new in 1961 with 64 seats, and marked a change of bodybuilder to Northern Counties. Similar 80 (80 NVO) arrived in 1962, but was an air-braked PD3/4 model. All subsequent double-deckers were to low-height layout without a sunken gangway, and included five Albion Lowlanders that were badged as Leylands, followed by Atlanteans, Fleetlines and finally Olympians. Leyland PD3 number 76 was written-off in an accident in 1977, but thankfully similar bus 80 is now in preservation.

(T C Bassindale [The Transport Museum, Wythall])

In 1915 J Hornsby began using two small buses on a service from Ashby to Scunthorpe, replacing them in 1921 with bigger vehicles. At this time the fleet-name Primrose Motors was in use and remained until about 1950. In 1948, an ex-Manchester Corporation Crossley was acquired, the first of many double-deckers to be added to this fleet. The fleet of Central Coaches, of Ashby, was acquired in 1959 followed by Harley's of Scotter a few years later, the latter bringing with it a stage service. Subsequently an interesting selection of double-deckers were acquired including AEC Regent Vs from Western Welsh and Rhondda, and an AEC Renown from City of Oxford plus some early examples of Leyland Atlanteans from Ribble and Maidstone and District. Only one new double-decker was ever purchased, a Roe-bodied Atlantean AN68 in 1977.

From the 1980s Fleetlines were also acquired from West Midlands PTE and London Transport. At this time there were three stage-carriage services all jointly run with Lincolnshire Road Car Company, and the Ashby to Scunthorpe was normally the preserve of double-deckers. CHG 550C is seen at the garage in September 1984, and was one of nine Leyland PD2A/27s purchased from Burnley and Pendle in 1976, although they immediately resold seven of these. CHG 550C has an East Lancs body and dates from 1965. When withdrawn from service, it went on to become a mobile snack bar back in Lancashire by 1986, but went for scrap in 1992. Hornsby Travel Services still trade in 2015, and operate a fleet of modern saloons and coaches.

*(Cliff Essex)*

James Dodds began running in 1912 between Troon and Ayr, and by 1930 had formed a new operators association with seven members. Working on the Ayr to Ardrossan route, in 1931 this became A.A. Motor Services Ltd, with Dodds of Troon as the largest member. During WWII a lot of extra contract work was found and double-deckers first appeared, later becoming used on the Ayr to Ardrossan route from 1946. The post-war years witnessed further expansion of services as the areas around Irvine and Prestwick developed and the Dodds fleet grew in size. Dodds was a very keen Guy user and took many Arab double-deckers into stock until the early 1970s, including a few new examples up to 1962. The Daimler Fleetline then became the double-decker of choice from

1964. By the late 1960s, A.A. Motor Services was down to three members, while in 1972 Robert Tumilty of Irvine sold out with his vehicles being split between Dodds and Young. D.T. No. 21 (AAG 648B) was a Northern Counties-bodied Daimler Fleetline that passed to Dodds from Tumilty and ran until 1980 when Dodds cannibalised it for spares. The other bus in this view is ENW 980D, the last half-cab purchased by Dodds and the only AEC Regent V to operate for A.A. It is a 1966 thirty-foot monocontrol model, new to Leeds City Transport (980) and acquired from West Yorkshire PTE in 1976. It has a 70-seat Roe body and following withdrawal in 1979 was sold for preservation. They are seen at Dodds' depot in Troon on 28 May 1978.

*(John Jones)*

The well-known independent G W Osborne and Sons was based in the Essex village of Tollesbury close to the River Blackwater and approximately twelve miles from Colchester. Shortly after the First World War a daily service to Colchester was introduced, followed in 1922 by one to Maldon and in 1930 to Witham. The first double-decker, a Daimler CWA6 utility, appeared in 1944 and was purchased new. A variety of double-deckers, all to low-bridge layout, appeared in the post war years and included a brand new AEC Regent III in 1950 and 2046 F, a Park Royal-bodied AEC Regent V in May 1957. The Regent V was the final new double-decker and lasted with Osborne's until February 1973. It is seen here at Colchester in August 1971, and after its sale was subsequently exported to the United States. Although this was the only AEC Regent V to be owned, Osborne's did later purchase three former AEC demonstrators, two Bridgemasters and a Renown. Osborne's soon became the envy of many independents in the area when in 1965 they opened a brand new garage and workshop at Tollesbury. Used double-deckers continued to feature in the fleet and included two former Scottish Bus Group Bristol VRTs and both the Bristol VRX prototypes, before settling down to a mixture of more mundane Leyland Atlanteans and Daimler Fleetlines. Osborne's was taken over by Suffolk-based independent Hedingham and District in 1997, in a deal which included the modern garage premises at Tollesbury.

*(Cliff Essex)*

The immaculate black and cream buses of F Lockey and Sons Ltd were a familiar sight in the Bishop Auckland area of County Durham for many years. Allegedly, this colour was chosen to make Lockey's vehicles stand out when parked amongst other buses and coaches. Operations began back in 1927 based in St Helens Auckland close to West Auckland, and running a service from Bishop Auckland to Evenwood, alongside but not jointly with OK Motor Services. Lockey was also engaged in private hire and contract work in the area and after acquiring a business at Shotton Colliery near Peterlee in 1954, they were to become involved in express work too. In 1958 Lockey bought JXN 371/8, a pair of former London Transport RTLs, while in 1963 these were joined by HLW 180, a former London Transport RT-type Regent. Coaches and saloons

also featured in the fleet, but the small number of double-deckers operated was always very interesting and often came via the OK fleet. A rare Daimler CSG6-30 of Leicester City Transport origin was joined by two forward-entrance AEC Regent Vs. KCK 880 was a 1958 Leyland PD3/4 that had a full-fronted Burlingham body complete with forward-entrance and sliding door. It had been purchased from Ribble Motor Services in 1974 and is seen in Bishop Auckland on 8 June 1978. KCK 880 lasted until 1979 and was later sold for conversion into a towing vehicle by a preservation group. The Lockey business passed to OK Motor Services in 1983, and was operated as a separate fleet until being fully-absorbed in 1985.

*(John Jones)*

The Wulfrunian was an unusual and innovative vehicle, but sadly a disastrous and costly mistake for its builder Guy Motors. However the pair delivered to Accrington Corporation in the autumn of 1961, 156/7 (35/6 VTF), were most peculiar to say the least, and quite unlike any other Wulfrunians built. They were the only examples with rear-entrance bodies, in this case by East Lancs with seating for 66. This pair had the smaller Gardner 6LW engine, mounted centrally and not offset, a ZF four-speed manual gearbox and were based on a 28-foot chassis. They did however feature air-suspension and disc brakes in common with the standard Wulfrunian and had Cave-Browne-Cave heating. They were not a success at Accrington and were withdrawn and sold in March 1968 to Ronsway Coaches of Hemel Hempstead. From here they parted company with 36 VTF soon moving on to Biss Bros, Bishops Stortford, ending its days with Spencer of High Wycombe who, after less than a year, sold it for scrap in July 1971. 35 VTF, on the other hand, passed in October 1969 to Byley Garage and Stores Ltd, who hailed from the Cheshire village of Byley, two and a half miles north of Middlewich. We see 35 VTF at Northwich in June 1971. It fared only slightly better here than its sister bus, being sold by Byley Garage in February 1972 for scrap.

*(Cliff Essex colletion)*

Based in the West Yorkshire town of Mirfield to the west of Dewsbury, John James Longstaff and Sons commenced operations in 1925 with a service to Dewsbury. The first double-decker arrived in 1947, a Burlingham-bodied Leyland PD1 and a limited company J J Longstaff and Sons Ltd was formed in 1948. Subsequent double-deckers were AEC Regents including examples from London Transport and Devon General. A rare Daimler CSG6-30 was acquired from Cunningham's of Paisley in 1967, and was duly replaced in 1972 by a new Daimler Fleetline with Roe bodywork and a Leyland engine. Ten years later this smart Northern Counties-bodied long-wheelbase Leyland Atlantean AN68C/2R was to replace the Fleetline. VCX 340X is seen in Dewsbury bus station on 22 September 1986 and itself was later replaced by a second-hand MCW Metrobus Mk2. The main stage-carriage route was from Dewsbury to Mirfield Ings via Knowle which for many years was operated in co-ordination with Joseph Wood and Yorkshire Woollen District. Longstaff always kept a small number of saloons, and latterly these became the regular service bus choice. The original premises were at Flash Lane in Mirfield, but these later moved to Shillbank Lane. Longstaff gave up its coaching operation in 2007 and eventually in December 2011, its bus service passed to Albert Lyles and Son of Batley.

*(Andrew Wiltshire)*

**Doncaster variety.** In 1923 Thomas Severn based in Stainforth began operating buses between Doncaster and Thorne Moorends running via Barnby Dun and Stainforth. This was a joint service with Samuel Morgan, Robert Store and Doncaster Corporation. By 1931 a second service from Doncaster to Stainforth was held and the fleet stood at around ten vehicles, and until the outbreak of WWII, Severn used the fleet-name Cressy. After the war new Leyland Titans of PD1 and PD2 variety completed the modernisation of the fleet by 1951, and in 1954 modern purpose-built premises were opened in nearby Dunscroft. Further new double-deckers in the shape of more Leyland PD2s and the first of six Roe-bodied PD3s were then added to stock. The first pair were acquired in 1958 as UWU 515/6, and these were PD3/5 models with Pneumocyclic transmission. UWU 516 has been posed for the photographer at the Dunscroft garage on 7 April 1974. It was withdrawn in February 1975 and sold for further service in Scotland. Between 1961 and 1964 four PD3/4 models with manual gearboxes and Roe forward-entrance bodywork were added to the fleet, to be followed in 1965 by the first of many Leyland Atlanteans. During the 1970s Severn usually operated around a dozen double-deckers, supplemented by a saloon and a few coaches. The Severn fleet passed to the South Yorkshire PTE in March 1979 together with seventeen passenger vehicles and the Dunscroft premises.

*(Malcolm Keeley)*

Samuel Morgan, who traded as Gwen, ran on the Doncaster to Armthorpe service in the 1920s alongside Robert Store who traded as Reliance. By the end of the decade Morgan wished to retire and Store expressed an interest in his licences. Store failed to obtain these, and the Morgan business passed to Richard Wilson whose Blue Line fleet also ran on the Armthorpe route. In 1949 Store retired and this business also passed to Richard Wilson, and a holding company was established. The Blue Line fleet continued to be based at Armthorpe and its main route was along the Doncaster to Goole corridor also serving Stainforth and Dunscroft. Guy double-deckers were very popular for years, many being bought new with the last example arriving in 1968, after which the Daimler Fleetline became the standard bus. In 1968 Blue Line obtained DUG 166/7C, Leyland PD3As from Kippax and District that were just three years old, and these remained in the fleet until the end. They had Roe 73-seat bodies and DUG 166C is seen here at the Armthorpe premises on 29 March 1978, alongside a fairly new Fleetline TET 745S. The end came in March 1979 when operations of both Samuel Morgan Ltd (Blue Line) and R Store Ltd (Reliance) passed to the South Yorkshire PTE. DUG 166C soon became a training bus (M100) for SYPTE while DUG 167C was later cut down for use as a tow-wagon and was ultimately sold for preservation.

*(Andrew Wiltshire)*

In 1928, Leonard Heath and E A Heath of Doncaster parted company, with Leonard setting up Leon Motor Services at Blaxton near Finningley. By 1937 he had relocated to premises in Finningley which was historically part of Nottinghamshire, and later moved to an ex RAF site adjacent to the airfield. Leon operated a service from Doncaster to Blaxton jointly with T S Madeley, a business which Leon then acquired in 1950. The first double-decker arrived in 1941 and thereafter, an impressive variety of vehicles entered the fleet. These included Crossleys, former London RTs, AEC Regent III and V models, Leyland PD2s and a number of Daimlers. An unusual Daimler CD650-30, a former experimental chassis of 1956 was acquired in 1961 and received a new Roe body appearing as 57 (432 KAL). The first completely new double-decker

appeared in 1972, a Roe-bodied Daimler Fleetline and would be the first of several bought new, together with a large number of used examples purchased from 1977 onwards. The example seen here in the depot yard on 29 March 1978 is 86 (JVO 815N), new in October 1975 with a 78-seat Roe body. The attractive livery was in use for many years, and has been described as Cambridge blue and broken white. By the 1980s Leon was one of the last-surviving Doncaster-area independents, and with two routes was still operating out of the South bus station. The last two double-deckers bought new were a pair of Dennis Tridents in 2000, and in 2004 the Leon business was acquired by MASS of North Anston near Sheffield.

*(Andrew Wiltshire)*

The Felix fleet was well known for its immaculately turned-out buses. It had been founded in 1921 at premises in East Lane, Stainforth by Ernest Parish who was to be engaged on a service from Doncaster to Armthorpe from 1925, which was later extended to Thorne Moorends. This was jointly operated with a number of other independents. Parish did not actually run to Stainforth, and in 1930 moved his business to a new site at Dunsville near Hatfield. A maroon, crimson and cream livery was adopted fairly early on and featured a Felix the Cat cartoon emblem, which was eventually replaced by a Felix Motors Ltd fleet-name. Double-deckers featured quite early on and in the early post-war years these were AEC Regents and Leyland Titan PD1s and PD2s. During the 1950s AEC Regent IIIs were followed by the Regent V of which eight were eventually purchased up until 1966. The last four were thirty-foot models with Roe bodies and one of these is 43 (932 BWR), a 73-seater dating from 1962, seen at the Christchurch terminus in Doncaster in September 1965. Four Roe-bodied Daimler Fleetlines were delivered between 1969 and 1975, and Felix Motors was the first of the Doncaster independents to sell out to South Yorkshire PTE, when in April 1976 the then managing director decided to retire. A fleet of fifteen passenger vehicles passed to the PTE, most of which were taken into PTE stock. Today we have two former Felix AECs in preservation, a Regent V and a Reliance, to remind us of this once very smart fleet.

*(Cliff Essex)*

Blue Ensign was the only Doncaster area independent actually based in the town itself, and was the smallest of all the fleets. Its history from the beginning was not particularly straightforward, but we know that George Ennifer commenced operating in 1922. By 1932 the title of the business was Ennifer and Farmer Ltd, and during the 1920s and 1930s the small fleet consisted mainly of Thornycroft, AEC and Leyland chassis. From 1934 the title G H Ennifer Ltd was in use and the trading name Blue Ensign appeared. The first double-decker was an ex Leeds Leyland TD2 that was acquired in 1946. A very rare AEC Q double-decker of London origin graced the fleet for a few years, as did FDT 202, a splendid Crossley DD42/7, which we see in Doncaster in June 1962. It was new to Blue Ensign in March 1948 and had a rare Scottish Commercial body. There later followed in 1954 a four-year old AEC Regent III with a Roe body that came from Doncaster Corporation. Two very smart Roe-bodied AEC Regent Vs with forward entrances arrived in 1959 and 1964, the latter replacing the Crossley. A Daimler Fleetline was purchased in 1967, while the last double-deckers purchased were two more Fleetlines in 1975, which replaced the two Regent Vs. Blue Ensign Coaches Ltd sold out to South Yorkshire PTE in April 1978, the deal included the three Fleetlines and three Bedford coaches.

*(Cliff Essex)*

Most of the Doncaster independents specified Roe bodywork on their new double-deckers as this coachbuilder seemed to specialise in supplying orders for just one or two vehicles to the smaller independent fleets. Rossie Motors Ltd was established by William Morpus in 1923 and was based in Rossington, a former mining village on the main East Coast railway line to the south east of Doncaster. His first vehicle was a 14-seat Ford which he ran for about four years, by which time the fleet had grown to four buses. The first double-decker was a Daimler CP6 of 1932 which joined the fleet in 1944, followed in 1945 by another CP6 and a Leyland TD2. The first new double-decker arrived in June 1949, a Barnard-bodied Daimler CVD6, and was followed by further new Daimlers including a rare CD650 with Burlingham body in 1953. Equally rare was this CVD6-30 model fitted with a Roe 73-seat forward-entrance body. 220 AWY was new in June 1962 and is seen at Rossington on 7 April 1974. A similar looking, CVG6-30 model was purchased in 1964, after which Rossie Motors went on to buy three Fleetlines between 1972 and 1976. The business passed to South Yorkshire PTE in December 1980, the deal included 220 AWY which became 1160 with its new owner, and eventually passed into preservation.

*(Malcolm Keeley)*

Robert Store began working the Doncaster to Stainforth route in 1922 initially with a new Ford 12-seater, but soon added larger buses including Chevrolets and Reos. The fleet-name Reliance was adopted, and in 1926 the route was extended to Goole and run jointly with Samuel Morgan. The business was registered in 1934 as R Store Ltd and in 1940 the first double-decker was acquired. This was a front-entrance Metro-Cammell-bodied AEC Q from Leeds City Transport that had originally been a demonstrator. It lasted until 1949 by which time Guy Arabs both single and double-deck were being added to the fleet. In April 1949 R. Store Ltd sold out to Richard Wilson who already owned Samuel Morgan's Blue Line fleet, and the two operations became associated businesses thereafter. The Roe-bodied Fleetline was chosen as a successor to the Guy Arab, and two Gardner-powered examples HWW 775/6J were delivered to Reliance (Store) in March 1971, with Blue Line receiving identical HWW 763/4J. They were 78-seaters and Reliance took a third similar bus in 1975. In 1977 the last new buses for Reliance were a further pair of Fleetlines, badged as Leylands, and featuring 76-seat Roe bodywork with attractive Leeds-style roof domes. One of these is TET 748S, noted leaving Doncaster in the morning rush hour of 29 March 1978.

*(Andrew Wiltshire)*

As mentioned on page 10, Harold Wilson's Premier fleet was based at East Lane in Stainforth, although Premier never actually ran a service to the village. A new Leyland Atlantean was acquired in 1973, followed by the first second-hand double-deckers in thirty three years, a pair of AECs. These were an ex City of Oxford Bridgemaster and a Regent V from Sheffield. Noted in Premier's yard on 18 April 1979 is BRB 493B, thought to be the only example of a Bristol FLF to appear with any of the Doncaster-area independents. This smartly turned-out bus is a FLF6G model dating from 1964 and was new to Midland General, and

had been acquired by Premier in October 1978. Just over two years later it was broken up at Barnsley, but by the end of 1981 the Premier fleet contained two more used Bristols. These being youthful VRTLL models from Tayside Regional Transport, and dating from 1977. During the 1980s the works contracts declined but Premier (Harold Wilson Ltd) soldiered on as the sole-remaining independent on the Doncaster to Thorne service. The end came in June 1988 when the business passed to South Yorkshire Transport along with five double-deckers, a saloon and several coaches.

*(Andrew Wiltshire)*

**Scottish Operators.** The history of the Ayrshire Bus Owners (A1 Service) Ltd can be traced back to early 1920s when there were over sixty small operators working in the area between Largs in the north, Ayr in the south and Kilmarnock in the east. In 1925, representatives from Ayrshire went to Lanarkshire to study the operations of an Owners Association, and reported favourably such that, the following year, a similar venture was established in Ayrshire. The A1 Service name was used and it began running between Ardrossan and Kilmarnock, with about a dozen members but, within a year, this had grown to forty. A limited company was formed in 1931 at which time membership stood at twenty-two. The variety of vehicles acquired by members was vast, but all were supposed to carry the basic fleet livery of blue, white and maroon. A particularly well known vehicle in the A1 Service fleet from the 1950s was NTF 9 of 1951, which had been acquired from Leyland Motors in 1956 by Docherty of Irvine. An all-Leyland 56-seater, NTF 9 is the unique PD2/15 with its pneumocyclic gearbox and air-brakes, having been built as a demonstration chassis. Docherty rejoined the Ayrshire Bus Owners (A1 Service) Ltd in 1957, and NTF 9 remained in use with them until the 1970s, after which it was considered a preserved vehicle. In 2015 it remains in preservation with Edward Docherty. It is seen here in Irvine in June 1972.

*(Cliff Essex)*

In 1960 T D Alexander, a Yorkshire independent operator from the Sheffield area, applied for the licences of J D McGibbon of Liff who ran from Dundee to Muirhead. In 1961 he took over Hunter and Nelson of Arbroath which included the Arbroath town services. T D Alexander (Greyhound Luxury Coaches) occupied Victoria Garage in Union Street East, Arbroath, and also had a garage in Dundee, and painted the vehicles in a red and cream livery. Both saloons and double-deckers were operated and there was plenty to interest the enthusiast in the fleet over the years. Double-deckers were all acquired as used vehicles, and included Guy Arabs, Bristol Ks, Leyland PD1s and PD2s. Vehicles would often move between the operation in Arbroath and that in Sheffield. The bus in this image in September 1966 is CCN 162, a Leyland PD2/1 dating from 1951 and fitted with a 56-seat Leyland body. It was one of nine PD2s purchased from Gateshead and District in 1966, some of which may have been allocated to the Sheffield fleet, and most had been withdrawn by the end of the decade. From the 1970s double-deckers began to diminish in the fleet as lightweight saloons became popular. Later double-deckers included AEC Regent Vs, a Daimler CCG6, Leyland PD2As and at least one PD3 as well as the inevitable Leyland Atlantean. The fleet was acquired by Tayside Public Transport Ltd in 1991, the Sheffield operation having been discontinued about twenty years earlier.

*(Cliff Essex)*

The photographer, visiting the Clyde on a short break from Cardiff, apparently stumbled across this former Western Welsh AEC Bridgemaster in a yard in Greenock on 21 April 1973. PBO 686 was new in January 1959, and was one of a batch of twenty similar buses that served their original owner until 1971. Most went for further service, but this was the only one to find a new home in Scotland, passing to Doig's Tours (Greenock) Ltd in September 1971. Alexander Doig, originally a coal merchant, began operations in 1909, and by the 1920s was running a service from Greenock to Largs. Eventually there were three services, though these were sold in 1931. A Glasgow operator, McDowall, purchased the business in 1960 and traded as Doig's Tours Ltd until 1965, when Doig's Tours (Greenock) Ltd was registered. Coaching was now the main business and some modern vehicles were acquired in the late 1960s into the 1970s, including a number of Plaxton-bodied Leyland Leopards. Another double-decker owned by Doig for a period was BGM 96 an ex Central SMT Bristol LD6G of 1960, and this together with PBO 686 were used on private hire and schools duties. In this view PBO 686 boldly advertises its owners express services to destinations in Ireland. The bus was sold to a dealer in February 1976 and almost certainly scrapped, while the Doig business eventually closed down for good in April 1991.

*(The late Les Ring)*

Garelochhead Coach Services Ltd was another fascinating operator, that went out of business over thirty years ago. They operated a large fleet of buses and coaches from their base in Garelochhead, a village situated at the north end of Gare Loch near Helensburgh. Coaches and saloons always formed the larger portion of the fleet, but the double-deck contribution was never the less interesting. JGD 675 was a splendid Foden PVD6 former demonstrator with Scottish Aviation bodywork that Garelochhead purchased in 1951. Other used vehicles included former London Transport RTs and an RTL in the 1960s plus a few Leyland PD2s from Trent. Double-deckers purchased new in 1957/58 were AEC Regent Vs 27/8 with Alexander rear-entrance bodies, followed in 1960 by 32 (LSN 286) a rare thirty-foot Daimler CSG6 appearing as an unregistered

exhibit at the 1959 Scottish Motor Show. In 1964 they took delivery of Regent V 43 (SSN 128) with unusual Northern Counties 64-seat fully-fronted forward entrance bodywork. Three further Regent Vs (46, 49 and 78), but to normal half-cab layout were received between 1965 and 1968, with 78 being the last half-cab to enter service in Scotland. Rear engine double-deckers were then introduced from 1971 to 1973 and included a Leyland Atlantean and three Daimler Fleetlines. The last pair had Alexander AL 74-seat bodies and were numbered 107/8 (GSN 514/5L). 108 is seen in Helensburgh on 29 May 1978. Operations ceased in 1980 after key MoD contracts were lost, while the stage services were already in decline.

*(John Jones)*

In 1933 McGill's Bus Services Ltd, of Barrhead, introduced their first service from Barrhead to Paisley and in 1939 the double-deck bus made its debut. There was further service expansion between 1953 and 1959 with new routes from Glenburn and Auchenback to Paisley and another from Barrhead to Renfrew. What was a small coach operation was closed down in 1965 and thereafter the fleet was to remain entirely double-deck until 1976. Early on, the double-deck fleet was varied and quite interesting with examples of AEC, Daimler, Guy and Leyland represented. A Cravens-bodied RT came from London Transport while a trio of Daimler CVG6s included a thirty-foot former demonstrator. Four wartime Guy Arabs received new Massey bodies in 1955 while a new Leyland PD2 received in 1959 also had an attractive Massey body. McGill's purchased VHS 501 an early Daimler Fleetline in 1963 and this had a 76-seat Northern Counties body, whereas all later Fleetlines had Alexander bodywork. This bus gave good service, outlasting many newer Fleetlines, and was eventually withdrawn for cannibalisation. On a very damp summer's day on 19 August 1981, VHS 501 is captured at the Paisley terminus about to depart for Barrhead. Originally McGill's used a red, grey and maroon livery for many years but the maroon was gradually phased out.

*(Andrew Wiltshire)*

From 1972 A.A. Motor Services with their head office in Ayr, continued with just two members, J B Young of Ayr and Dodds of Troon. The smart green and cream livery was distinctive and Dodds opted to use dark green as a third colour on its buses. Unlike Dodds, Young had a modern garage adjacent to Ayr bus station, large enough to keep all vehicles under cover. Young was an enthusiastic Leyland user and in the post war years bought mainly new vehicles, comprising examples of Royal Tiger, Tiger Cub and Leopard saloons. For double-deckers all-Leyland PD2s were followed by an Alexander-bodied example and a solitary PD3/1 with Northern Counties-body in 1960. In 1965 Young purchased its first Leyland Atlantean, CSD 344C, a smart 77-seat example with Northern Counties bodywork. This was followed by similar EAG 267D in 1966, and which we see here in Ayr on 28 May 1978. The bus was withdrawn two years later and became a temporary waiting room at Ayr, being sold for scrap locally in 1981. In 1972 Young received Scotland's first Leyland National, XSD 789L, and this model gradually became the standard purchase for Young as they moved away from double-deckers. *(John Jones)*

Massey Bros of Pemberton produced some fine-looking double-deck bodies during the 1950s and 1960s and specialised in smaller orders often for single vehicles for both municipal and independent fleets. They were slow to produce a body for rear-engine chassis and it was 1964 when they completed a solitary Daimler Fleetline for A1 Service. All subsequent rear-engine bodies were on Leyland Atlantean chassis, the two main customers being Maidstone and Colchester Corporations. Maidstone took twenty similar buses between 1965 and 1968, but these had short lives in that town, as a change in policy saw all double-deckers replaced by lightweight saloons from the mid-1970s onwards. JKE 340E was new in March 1967 and part of a batch of eight acquired to replace Maidstone's trolleybuses, when the system was finally abandoned in May 1967. This bus, together with JKE 341E, was sold to bus dealer Ensign in March 1977, and passed to Rapson of Brora later the same month. JKE 340E is seen on 2 June 1978 at Latheron, a village in Caithness where the Thurso and Wick roads diverge. Sister bus JKE 341E did not stay in Scotland very long, passing on to Osborne Tollesbury by January 1978. JKE 340E remained with Rapson until 1980, passing to Kerr, Galston, Ayrshire by August that year, and was still owned in April 1986. *(John Jones)*

We now pay a visit to Lanarkshire which was home to a number of independent operators including William Irvine, of Law, and not to be confused with John Irvine, of nearby Salsburgh. Law was a former mining village situated between Carluke and Wishaw, and it was between these two towns that Irvine operated stage service 48. For many years Irvine's buses and coaches, turned out in a distinctive maroon, red and cream livery, could be found plying this route. A great variety of both double-deckers and saloons were purchased and included this 1963 Leyland Atlantean HXS 85 which is seen in Law on 18 May 1980. It has an Alexander body and was new to Graham's Bus Service, of Paisley, as their number 61, being sold by them in July 1979. It was withdrawn by Irvine's about a month after this photograph was taken. Double-deckers operated over the years included an ex City of Oxford AEC Regent V acquired in 1970 and a former South Shields Daimler CSG6 in 1972. By 1980 half-cabs were still in evidence in the form of ASC 668B, an ex-Lothian Leyland PD3, while FKY 243E was Leyland PD3A that was new to Bradford Corporation Transport, and which Irvine's had acquired from nearby operator Wilson's of Carnwath. Leyland Atlanteans continued to be popular for a number of years although Fleetlines were also tried including a number of former London Transport examples. Irvine's withdrew from local service operations at the beginning of August 2012, and ceased to operate altogether, after serving the Lanarkshire village and surroundings for more than half a century.

*(John Jones)*

A & C McLennan, of Spittalfield, was a well-known and interesting independent operator from Perthshire and was founded in 1945. They operated a number of routes in the area including Spittalfield to Perth and Dunkeld to Blairgowrie. Used double-deckers featured from an early stage and elderly Leyland TDs and Daimlers were popular, often being rebuilt by McLennan. Other acquisitions included a number of former London Transport RTLs while a Guy Wulfrunian was used in the early 1970s. In 1957 McLennan acquired XG 8205, a former Middlesbrough Corporation Transport Leyland PD1 with Roe 56-seat bodywork that had been new in March 1946. They numbered it 81 and fitted platform doors. In 1958 a further two examples from the same batch of six buses, XG 8202/4 were acquired, and took fleet numbers 96 and 97, also receiving platform doors. This pair were withdrawn in 1966 and 1964 respectively, while 81 (XG 8205) lasted until March 1967. It is seen at Spittalfield in the company of some ex London Transport RTLs on 28 July 1966. After withdrawal it remained derelict on the premises until at least 1974. The end came in 1985 when McLennan's sold out to another private fleet, Stagecoach of Perth, which then saw Stagecoach expand into local bus operation for the first time. The rest is history.

*(Malcolm Keeley)*

Rennies of Dunfermline Ltd was established in 1948 and based in Cairneyhill west of Dunfermline. Their red and cream buses were heavily used on contract work in the area which had a number of collieries and naval dockyard at Rosyth. The first double-decker, an ex Doncaster Corporation low-bridge Guy Arab arrived in 1958, and subsequently a vast number of double-deckers passed through the fleet some only staying with Rennies for a few months, before being sold on or scrapped. JCK 532 was a Leyland PD2/12 dating from 1956 that had come from Ribble (1457), along with three others in 1972. It had a 61-seat Burlingham body with platform doors. None stayed for long in the Rennie fleet and JCK 532 had been withdrawn by the end of 1973. Amongst the other double-deckers that Rennie purchased in the 1960s and 1970s were Southdown Leyland TD5s, Chesterfield Daimler CVG6s, East Midland Leyland PD3s, a Standerwick Atlantean, Chester Guy Arab IVs and a former South Wales Transport AEC Bridgemaster. The 1980s were also interesting as Rennie took in Atlanteans, Dennis Dominators and a huge fleet of MCW Metropolitans. After deregulation in 1986, some stage-carriage work commenced, but this did not last long. Proprietor Jack Rennie retired in 2007, and the business was sold to Stagecoach East Scotland.

*(Andrew Wiltshire collection)*

Clyde Coast Services Ltd was another association of bus owners that operated in Ayrshire. They were the smallest cooperative and formed in around 1928 or 1929 when several members broke away from Ayrshire Bus Owners (A1 Service). They operated just one route along the Clyde coast between Largs and Saltcoats via West Kilbride and Ardrossan. Up until the 1960s there were four members Frazer, Hogarth, McGregor and Shields, but by 1977 just Frazer and McGregor survived based at garages in Fairlie and Saltcoats respectively. Double-deckers first appeared in 1941, the War having created extra demand for capacity, and apart from a new Leyland PD1 in 1946, all have been used acquisitions and included gems like former Ribble Leyland PD2s and London RTs. McGregor had three Crossley DD42s that came from Barrow in Furness Corporation in 1958 and two of them EO 8792/5 are seen here at Saltcoats Church in the mid-1960s, by which time, EO 8795 had been fitted with a Gardner engine. They date from 1948 and have Crossley 58-seat bodywork. Originally the Clyde Coast fleet wore a silver and blue livery but silver was later replaced by a more durable grey as seen on these two Crossleys. Saloons and coaches gradually took over from double-deckers, and the operation of the latter had ceased altogether by 1972. However this resumed again after deregulation when Olympians and Ailsas featured in the fleet. Clyde Coast's services passed to Stagecoach A1 Service in September 1995, but double-deckers were retained for schools contracts.

*(Cliff Essex collection)*

Clan Coaches based at Kyle of Lochalsh in north-west Scotland ran a fleet of coaches in the early 1980s. These included a number of former Glenton Tours centre-entrance AEC Reliances which were used on its well known Skye-Way service, which linked Skye with Glasgow. They also ran a small fleet of double-deckers on local school contracts and at least one saloon. The first double-deckers to arrive, both from Red and White, were 12 EWO in September 1975 and AAX 22B the following month, Bristol Lodekka FS6B models with ECW rear entrance bodies and platform doors. They were joined in September 1981 by another interesting Bristol Lodekka JMR 821F, an FLF that had been new in 1968 as the last double-decker delivered to Wilts and Dorset. It was one of five rare FLF6L models that featured a Leyland 0.600 engine, a variation only taken by four Tilling fleets. On 27 August 1977 we see one of the former Red and White Lodekkas, AAX 22B parked in very picturesque surroundings at Kyle of Lochalsh. With the eventual departure of the two Bristol FSs in the 1980s, another double-decker added to stock was former Leicester City Transport Leyland Atlantean PBC 111G.

*(Malcolm Keeley)*

Cunningham's Bus Service Ltd began operating in the 1920s on the relatively short but very lucrative route, between Paisley County Place and Renfrew Ferry which was run jointly with Paton Brothers of Renfrew. At Renfrew Ferry, they connected with the passenger and vehicle chain ferry to Yoker. Cunningham's green and white liveried vehicles were based at Underwood Garage in Paisley, in the shadow of the Glasgow to Gourock railway line, and was predominantly a double-deck fleet. The second-hand vehicles were always very interesting with many Leylands coming from fleets like Ribble, Edinburgh Corporation and Trent. The first new double-decker arrived in 1967, an Alexander-bodied Leyland Atlantean, and six more were to be acquired between 1972 and 1977. The last one of all was 71 (VGD 779R), an AN68A/1R model new in June 1977, one of a similar pair with attractive Roe 76-seat bodywork, and it is seen on 29 May 1978. The Cunningham's business was sold to Western SMT on 12 August 1979 though no vehicles were retained, the Atlanteans being sold on for further service. VGD 779R passed to neighbouring fleet Graham's Bus Service Ltd, of Paisley, where it became their L17, while sister bus 65 (LGA 18P) became Graham's L16.

*(John Jones)*

**Urban settings.** Green Bus, of Rugeley, is another fondly remembered south Staffordshire independent. It was founded by Charles J. Whieldon who adapted a van for passengers in the early 1920s, and was based in Hollington near Uttoxeter. In 1927 he began operating from Uttoxeter to Hednesford via Rugeley using a 20-seat Reo and in 1928 started a service to Lichfield, again via Rugeley. In 1934 operations moved to Rugeley and by 1939 the fleet stood at sixteen buses and included the first double-deckers, seven former Nottingham AEC Regents. Subsequent double-deckers included Guy Arabs and a few rare Fodens which were also a popular choice for saloons. By the 1960s there was a mix of AEC, Guy, Leyland and a few Daimlers including four CVG6 models acquired from Western SMT in 1965. 44 (BSD 468) dated from 1951 and had an Alexander low-bridge body, and was the last example to remain in service being withdrawn and sold for scrap in 1969. Green Bus bought a number of new Seddon saloons in the years 1969 to 1973, while the final preferred type of double-decker was the Bristol Lodekka. It has been reported that a new Leyland Atlantean was on order when Green Bus Company Ltd was taken over by Midland Red in November 1973.

*(T C Bassindale [The Transport Museum, Wythall])*

Having been involved operating with his father and uncle, Frank Procter of Longton began operating as a solo concern in 1922, jointly on the Hanley to Leek route. In 1929 he formed an alliance with A Walker of Longton and moved to premises at Leek Road, Hanley in 1932. Double-deckers were first introduced from 1950, and saw a trio of former Birmingham City Transport utility Daimlers enter service. The business became F Procter and Sons Ltd in 1951, and further used double-deckers were added to the fleet including more Daimlers and two former London Transport RTs with Craven bodies. A Massey-bodied CVD6 GBW 336, was followed by an ex City of Oxford AEC Regent III. The first of several rear-engined double-deckers 4559 VC was purchased in 1964, a former

demonstration Daimler Fleetline. Two new examples with low-height Alexander bodies followed in 1965 and 1968. GBF 279N seen in Hanley on 17 April 1979 was a Leyland Atlantean, one of a pair new in late 1974. It had a 76-seat Alexander body built to a standard Greater Glasgow PTE design. The last double-decker purchased was a former Tayside Bristol VRTLL, which saw that operator's livery adopted by Procter and applied to the two 1974 Atlanteans. By now Procter was based at modern premises in Fenton and coaching had become the main part of the business. However, they still maintained the service 16 from Hanley to Leek using saloons until March 2013, when the whole bus and coaching operation was suddenly closed down.

*(John Jones)*

Hadley Coaches was a small operator from Quarry Bank, a village in the West Midlands, who it is thought commenced trading in about 1964. They kept a fleet of coaches and had at least two double-deckers which were used for school contracts and works services. One of these was XHA 475, a BMMO D7 with a 63-seat four-bay Metro-Cammell body that was new to Midland Red at Sutton Coldfield as 4475. The BMMO D7 was a Midland Red lightweight design that was introduced in 1953, and a total of 350 were built up to 1957. XHA 475 was withdrawn in September 1971 passing to Green of Brierley Hill in February 1972. They did not use it and sold it to Hadley by April that year. Green also ran two other BMMO D7s, THA 82 and 759 BHA, a rare occurrence, as only a handful of D7s saw any further service after Midland Red. XHA 475 is seen sharing Hadley's depot yard in New Street in May 1972 with EAX 967C, an ex Hills of Tredegar Duple-bodied Ford 570E, and carries an unusual pale blue/grey livery. The D7 passed back to Green once more in December 1974, and survived with them until withdrawal in October 1977. Readers who would like to see a BMMO D7 in 2015 should visit the Transport Museum at Wythall near Birmingham where a similar 4482 (XHA 482) is on display in Midland Red livery.

*(Cliff Essex)*

We now take a look at a well-known Leicestershire independent. It was in 1920 that John Stinson Astill commenced a route from the village of Ratby into the centre of Leicester using a converted truck which he had been using to carry coal. He was joined by Thomas Jordan in 1924 to form Astill and Jordan Ltd. Until 1930 the route ran via Braunstone Cross Roads, but was then changed to run via Glenfield and Groby Road to compete with Midland Red. From this time a number of new vehicles were purchased. The early post-war period witnessed the arrival of a pair of rare Vulcans whilst the first double-decker arrived in 1956, a former East Yorkshire Leyland TD5 with an ECW body. Double-deck operation ceased from 1972, but returned by 1978 as loadings increased once more, and Astill and Jordan purchased a former Leicester City Transport Leyland PD3A. Seen in Leicester in October 1982 is Alexander-bodied Leyland Atlantean 5 (JSC 862E) of 1967, that was previously Lothian Regional Transport 862. By 1985 the fleet comprised five Daimler Fleetlines of London Transport origin and the service to Ratby was now shared with Midland Fox and Hylton and Dawson. Astill and Jordan Ltd sold out to Midland Fox in November 1988.

*(Cliff Essex)*

W G Phillips' Bristol-based Eastville Coaches was in business by 1968, and by the early 1980s was based around a piece of land and a workshop at Redcliff Backs, which formed part of Bristol's floating harbour. During 1983 three double-deckers were taken into stock, all Alexander-bodied Leyland Atlanteans. Two of these included ex Lothian EWS 821D of 1967 which lasted for just eleven months, and from Tyne and Wear PTE, long-wheelbase GBB 523K, which had been rebuilt to single-door layout. Our image depicts the third acquisition, MDS 691P, which was acquired from Strathclyde PTE (LA1028) and is seen on 26 August 1983 at the Redcliff Backs parking ground. It was new in May 1976, and as can be seen, its Alexander body featured panoramic windows, which were problematic for its original owner. MDS 691P later worked in Cornwall before passing to north Wales independent Express of Penygroes in November 1995. Meanwhile Eastville Coaches later moved to Albert Crescent in the St Philips area of the city, and continued to purchase double-deckers. These included several Bristol VRTs, and from the late 1990s, a varied collection of Leyland Olympians. By 2009 Eastville were additionally using the Premier Travel name, and had become involved in running stage service 462 to Mangotsfield.

*(Andrew Wiltshire)*

Graham's Bus Service Ltd originally started operating in 1929 between Johnstone and Glasgow, as part of the South Western Bus Owners Cooperative. When this ended in 1932, they began working from Linwood to Paisley (Hawkhead), and acquired their first double-deckers in 1940, some Leyland TD1 and TD2 models from Glasgow Corporation. From 1944 the Guy Arab was the preferred choice for new double-deckers until 1963, although used examples continued to be added to stock after his date. Graham's became a limited company in 1953 and at this point the livery changed to orange and cream, while the fleet would be based at Hawkhead, Paisley. The new car factory at Linwood saw services expand from 1963, and this prompted the move to higher-capacity 78-seat rear-engine double-deckers. The Daimler Fleetline would be the standard type for this role until 1976, but a small number of Atlanteans were also obtained, both new and second-hand. D14 (NXS 14L) was one of three Fleetlines new in 1973 with Alexander 74-seat bodies and is seen in Paisley on 29 May 1978. From 1977 Graham's would again work into the centre of Glasgow, coinciding with the arrival of the first of four new Leyland Atlanteans, the last new double-deckers to be purchased. From 1979 Graham's then took advantage of many relatively youthful used Daimler Fleetlines from London Transport, before operations came to an end in April 1990.

*(John Jones)*

Chasetown is a former mining village in Staffordshire and rapidly grew after WWII having joined up with neighbouring Burntwood by the 1970s. H & M Coaches Ltd of Chasetown were in existence by this time running a small coach fleet and a number of double-deckers on schools contracts. These were known to have included three former East Kent Guy Arab IVs with Park Royal bodies (MFN 887/91/6), in the years 1972/73. By the late 1970s these had been replaced by BUF 273/4C, a pair of ex Southdown Motor Services Leyland PD3/4s. These were two of the well-known Southdown Queen Mary design, and were fitted with full-fronted Northern Counties 69-seat bodies, having formed part of a batch of thirty-five similar vehicles new in the spring of 1965. This view of BUF 274C was taken in Cannock on 23 March 1982 when it is thought that one of the regular haunts for the PD3s for a number of years was the school contract to Cardinal Griffin Catholic High School, Cannock. H & M Coaches operated until at least late 1991, but BUF 274C had by then been sold to become transport for workers on a berry farm at Inchture near Dundee. On the other hand BUF 273C became a mobile home with travellers by 1987, and possibly ended up in France.

*(John Jones)*

Bushey Heath is a neighbourhood of the Hertfordshire town of Bushey south-east of Watford. George Kirby was from Bushey Heath and in 1926 founded Kirby's Luxury Coaches which gained a fine reputation for its coaching services for many years. The business remained in family hands until 1964, after which under new management, it continued to serve the area and grew to become The Kirby Group. Kirby's coach fleet was augmented with the purchase of a number of double-deckers for contract work from dealer Passenger Vehicle Sales (PVS) of Silver End, Essex, from where he obtained four former South Wales Transport AECs. These were Bridgemasters RCY 371 and UCY 837 in March 1970 having previously spent a short spell with City Coach Lines of Upminster. The Bridgemasters including UCY 837, the subject of our photograph of August 1970, passed to Cinema Travel, Twickenham as non-PSVs in July 1972. UCY 837 ended up derelict in the yard of Denyer's Coaches, Stondon Massey in Essex by the late 1970s. The Kirby Group went out of business during the 1990s, but AEC Bridgemaster UCY 837 was rescued for preservation in October 2002 and returned to South Wales. After a lengthy restoration, it was back on the road in 2014.

*(Andrew Wiltshire collection)*

By 1977 the Ayrshire Bus Owners (A1 Service) was down to just fourteen members, but there was still a great number of interesting vehicles in the fleet. Services remained crew-operated and revenue was distributed fairly, while all members adhered to a strict duty cycle on the main Ardrossan to Kilmarnock service. The livery remained blue and cream with maroon as an optional third colour. Having moved away from front-engine double-deckers in the mid-1960s, rear engine Leyland Atlanteans and Daimler Fleetlines were the standard purchase usually with Alexander bodywork, but Northern Counties and even Massey bodies appeared. Some members continued to keep an eye out for good used vehicles often in the form of relatively low-mileage former demonstrators. With the announcement that Leyland would be discontinuing the Fleetline model, two members chose to order some East Lancs-bodied Dennis Dominators for 1979. Andrew Hunter of Dreghorn took a pair (ECS 58V and GSJ 60V) while McKinnon of Kilmarnock took ECS 59V. The latter is seen here in Irvine, bound for Kilmarnock on 21 August 1981. McKinnon, who incidentally also ran a milk tanker business from his premises, usually kept about seven operational buses at any one time, and in 1980 his fleet comprised two Atlanteans, four Fleetlines and the Dennis Dominator. He introduced a pair of Leyland Tiger saloons to his fleet in the early 1980s, and had moved to new premises in Kilmarnock at around this time too.

*(Andrew Wiltshire)*

Bill Thomas lived at Golden Valley, Staverton, between Cheltenham and Gloucester. In 1960 he purchased a small Gloucester-based minibus and taxi firm from a Mr Swann, and with it came the Swanbrook trading name. School contracts were soon acquired and larger vehicles were then needed. An interesting variety of buses and coaches were purchased and in 1969 the first double-deckers arrived. A stage-carriage service commenced in 1974 running from Gloucester to Tewkesbury, acquired from Cathedral Coaches of Gloucester. In 1981/82 a fleet of double-deckers was purchased from City of Nottingham Transport comprising seven Leyland Atlanteans and eight Daimler Fleetlines. In March 1982 Swanbrook acquired a small interest in South Wales independent CK Coaches (Cardiff) Ltd who were experiencing a vehicle crisis. Four of these double-deckers were then sent to Cardiff to help out. CK was a small coach firm that had been formed in 1974 by Keith Morris, and who since April 1981 had been running a number of stage services in Cardiff in direct competition with City of Cardiff Transport. The Swanbrook vehicles were brought in as a last-ditch attempt to keep services running, and MCW-bodied Atlantean JTV 493E is noted on Kingsway on 1 March 1982. CK ceased trading on 31 March 1982 and the six Swanbrook vehicles returned to Gloucestershire. Swanbrook still continues to trade in 2015.

*(Andrew Wiltshire)*

After the First World War, Heath Hayes a former mining village in Staffordshire, grew rapidly. Seizing an opportunity, in 1922 Cecil Harper purchased a Ford Model T van which could be adapted to carry passengers, and commenced running a service from Heath Hayes to Cannock. By 1932 the service had been extended south to Aldridge, with another service added from Cannock to Brewood. By then much larger Morris Dictators were in use. The first of many double-deckers was purchased in 1941, and by 1944 the fleet stood at twenty-six buses. In 1946 the Aldridge route was extended to Kingstanding. A mixture of new and used vehicles was acquired in the 1950s including Leyland and Daimler double-deckers from Birmingham Corporation Transport. Harper Brothers is remembered for the ex-London Transport RTs and RTLs as well as the former St Helens RT-type Regents and the many curious rebuilds it undertook. Their distinctive pale green livery adorned some smart new Leyland PD2s and PD3s in the 1960s, while in 1964 the route was extended from Kingstanding into the centre of Birmingham. The first of six Daimler Fleetlines was purchased in 1970 and one of these BRE 311J is seen heading into Birmingham on 10 March 1973. Beset by labour problems and increasing costs, Harper Bros (Heath Hayes) Ltd was acquired by Midland Red on 7 September 1974.

*(John Jones)*

This fine-looking Leyland PD3 has been posed for enthusiasts during a visit to the Radford premises of Skill's of Nottingham in September 1969. 780 DAU has Skill's fleet number 80 and was the second of two Leyland PD3/1s purchased by them in 1959, the other being 70 (570 CTO). They both had Metro-Cammell forward-entrance bodies with seating for 72 passengers and were used on a service to East Bridgford. Skill's began operating around 1919 with local works contracts and by 1927 had introduced express coach services from Nottingham to resorts on the east coast of England. Guy Arabs joined the rapidly expanding fleet as some of the first double-deckers. A large number of new vehicles were acquired in the early post-war years, and a new Daimler CVD6 with Duple

bodywork 10 (LTO 10) arrived in 1950, but two further examples were diverted to Gash of Newark. Second-hand double-deckers also featured in the 1950s and included a number of AECs. The pair of Leyland PD3s was sold to O.K. Motor Services of Bishop Auckland in September 1970, where they lasted in service a further three years. Double-deckers did not return to the Skill's fleet for nearly thirteen years, at which point a former Maidstone and District Volvo Ailsa was purchased for service bus work, and was later joined by similar examples of West Midlands PTE and Tayside origin. In 2015 Skill's is still in business based in Bulwell, Nottingham and concentrating mainly on coaching.

*(Cliff Essex)*

King Alfred Motor Services can be traced back to 1915, when Robert Chisnell began using small buses to ferry troops to and from camps in the Winchester area, and by 1922 was running two circular bus services to a new estate in the town. By the 1930s a network of services were being run by King Alfred throughout the city as well as to surrounding towns and villages. The first double-deckers were acquired in 1942, and two small operators were taken over in the early post-war period which allowed further expansion. The first of a fleet of sixteen new Leyland Titan double-deckers began to arrive from 1946, although a small number of new saloons were also acquired. A former AEC Regent V demonstrator was obtained in 1958, while in 1959 King Alfred returned to low-height buses with the first of four AEC Bridgemasters, followed in 1964 by a pair of AEC Renowns with Park Royal bodies. By the 1960s the business was struggling with passenger numbers falling and increased congestion on its routes. Despite this, four new 76-seat Roe-bodied Leyland Atlanteans were purchased in 1967 and one of these, HOR 590E, is noted in The Broadway, Winchester. The last new buses were a trio of revolutionary MCW Metro-Scania saloons in 1971. King Alfred sold out to Hants and Dorset Motor Services on 23 April 1971 and HOR 590E was included in the deal. The bus eventually passed to Bristol Omnibus who removed the roof and put it to work as an open-topper at Weston-super-Mare. After several subsequent owners, HOR 590E survives in preservation in 2015.

(Cliff Essex)

**Rebuilt or rebodied.** Possibly one of the most well-known independent fleets in the UK was Barton Transport which was based in the Nottingham area, but whose fleet could be encountered much farther afield. Barton's vehicles were always very interesting and unusual and many in-house rebuilds were carried out over the years using older chassis that still offered a few more years' service. Shortly after WWII Barton took a large number of Leyland PD1A double-deckers with smart Duple low-bridge bodies and forward entrances. This was the nearest the double-deck fleet came to standardisation, as subsequently small batches of used and new double-deckers appeared as well as a variety of rebuilds. The vehicle in this view taken in Nottingham on 14 June 1973 is 822 (822 DNN),

which was based on a Leyland PS1 single-deck chassis that received a new Northern Counties full-fronted 63-seat body in 1959. It would be the first of around sixteen similar-looking rebuilds from Barton's own workshops using various mechanical parts, and bodied by the Wigan-based coachbuilder. The Barton fleet started to change rapidly with the advent of the Bus Grant, and from the early 1970s the fascinating fleet of buses was gradually swept away by a large fleet of grant-specification Leyland Leopard and Bedford coaches. As for 822 DNN it was withdrawn and had been exported to the United States by 1975.

*(John Jones)*

Alongside their haulage business, the Hanson family began running charabancs in the Huddersfield area from about 1920, and started a bus service from 1924. From 1935 a network of local services were operated by Hansons Buses Ltd, some jointly run with Huddersfield Joint Omnibus Committee. The fleet expanded in the post-war years with the purchase of three coach fleets and it was during this period that the company undertook a number of major chassis rebuilds in its own workshops. Seven double-deckers were extensively rebuilt between 1956 and 1963, using various chassis parts from old AEC Regal and Regent chassis. The first three received new rear-entrance Roe bodywork between 1956 and 1958, while the last four were dealt with between 1961 and 1963 and featured new front-entrance Roe bodywork. The first of these is 361 (TVH 497) which is seen close to the Hanson garage in July 1968, with a rebuilt AEC saloon in the background. TVH 497 had started out in 1950 as an AEC Regal with a Duple body. Faced with the substantial cost of fleet replacement, James Hanson sold the buses and stage services to Huddersfield Corporation on 1 October 1969, continuing solely as a coach operator. The coach business passed to West Yorkshire PTE in 1974. As for TVH 497, it passed to Thornes of Bubwith in 1969 and was later sold for preservation, but sadly scrapped.

(Cliff Essex)

From 1944 the Guy Arab became a very popular choice in the Stainforth-based fleet of Reliance, even after 1949 when it was sold to R Wilson and was operated in close alliance with the Blue Line (Morgan) fleet at nearby Armthorpe. By 1967 fifteen reliable Guy Arabs of Mk I through to MkV had been purchased, nine of these being double-deckers. Seven of these were bought new and included a solitary Mk IV model with unusual Burlingham bodywork, and a trio of Mk Vs with Roe forward-entrance bodies. The two used Arabs were both Mk II models with Gardner 5LW engines. MNU 777 with a Northern Coachbuilders body dated from 1948 and had been new to E Naylor and Sons of South Normanton. The other bus was FPT 207 which is seen here at the Christchurch terminus in Doncaster in about 1964. It was new in 1943 to Sunderland and District and had a Pickering body. This was scrapped and replaced in 1953 with a 56-seat Roe body and passed to Reliance in January 1961. After seven years it was withdrawn and eventually sold for scrap in 1969. By 1972 there were just four Guys left in service, and three of these passed to South Yorkshire PTE on 29 March 1979 when Reliance ceased to trade. None of the Guys was operated by the PTE, but the five Fleetlines were retained.

(Cliff Essex collection)

VHO 123 was a double-decker with an interesting history. It was based on an AEC Regent III 9612A chassis dating from 1950 that was used by AEC as a test-bed. In 1959 it was sold to Liss and District and given a new 56-seat Roe low-bridge forward-entrance body, and duly appeared at the 1959 British Coach Rally at Brighton. A further example was 150 AOU, which was built in 1949 and again used by AEC as a test-bed until sale to Liss & District when it was bodied in February 1961 to full-front configuration. Both later passed to associated company Creamline of Bordon in east Hampshire and at some point VHO 123 moved on to the South Devon fleet Tally Ho! at Kingsbridge. The history of Tally Ho! can be traced back to 1926, and in 1960 while still based in East Allington, its blue and white coaches were acquired by the Wellington and Gullett families. It expanded by taking over a number of small operators and in 1971 moved to new premises at Kingsbridge. The same year saw Western National withdraw its services from the Kingsbridge area, and Tally Ho! began operating a network of low-frequency services in the area. Double-deckers were operated from 1964, and later included AEC Regent Vs, Daimler Fleetlines, Leyland Atlanteans and a number of Bristol VRTs. In this view AEC Regent III VHO 123 is seen in the South Hams area of Devon in June 1973 and it had been exported to the United States by 1976.

*(Cliff Essex)*

EVD 406 was a Crossley DD42/7 with Scottish Commercial 53-seat bodywork that had been delivered new in June 1949 to Baxters of Airdrie, Scotland. In August 1953 it passed to Joseph Wood of Mirfield near Dewsbury and was his first double-decker. Joseph Wood had founded his business in 1925 and was involved in operating the short twenty minute service from Dewsbury bus station to Mirfield via Knowle, alongside J J Longstaff also of Mirfield (see page 25 lower) and Yorkshire Woollen District. The body on EVD 406 was found to be in poor condition and was scrapped, the chassis being driven to Leeds to receive a new 56-sea Roe body re-entering service with Wood in April 1955. Upon his death the business passed to Alice Wood in 1963 but continued to trade as Joseph Wood and Sons. 20 (EVD 406) is seen in Dewsbury bus station in May 1964, and served Wood until 1970. The final double-decker to be operated was TGX 769M, an ex-London Transport Daimler Fleetline with a Park Royal body. Joseph Wood and Sons was taken over by the Traject Group of Huddersfield in July 1983 and placed under a newly-created company Gobig Ltd. They continued to operate Wood's share of the Mirfield service, but sold the Fleetline and used an Alexander-bodied Leyland Leopard that was interestingly built for service in Singapore. Meanwhile EVD 406 was retained for preservation by the Wood family, eventually being put back on to the road in 1999. After several changes of ownership it became part of the Dewsbury Bus Museum in 2014.

*(Cliff Essex collection)*

Based in Royal Leamington Spa, G & G Coaches was founded by two former Midland Red employees in 1954. Messrs Green and Griffin began using buses and coaches on contract work in the area and purchased their first double-decker in 1960. AECs and Leylands were always favoured, and especially noteworthy vehicles included former Midland Red all-Leyland PD2s SHA 448/56 of 1953, two of the much admired LD8 class, that G & G acquired in 1965. Equally as interesting were three double-deckers JUE 348/9/51, that G & G purchased from Midland Red in 1971. These were Leyland Tiger PS2/3 models of 1950, new to Stratford-upon-Avon Blue Motors and originally fitted with Willowbrook single-deck bodies. Stratford Blue had four of them re-bodied by Northern Counties as forward-entrance double-deckers in 1963. This view of JUE 348 was taken on 17 June 1973. It is pleasing to note that similar JUE 349 survives and is currently under restoration at The Transport Museum, Wythall in 2015. G & G coaches went on to purchase many more double-deckers including Atlanteans from the likes of Ribble, Brighton and Merseyside, not forgetting some MCW Metropolitan double-deckers in the late 1980s. After deregulation G & G became involved in stage-carriage work and the fleet expanded greatly. It was eventually taken over by Western Travel subsidiary Midland Red (South) in January 1990.

*(John Jones)*

By the early 1980s, Staffordshire independent Stevensons Bus Services continued to operate two main routes from Burton-upon-Trent and another to Ashbourne, a limited stop service to Birmingham, as well as some minor routes and Rugeley town services. Rear-engine double-deckers first appeared in 1975 in the form of ex Portsmouth Atlanteans and a number of former Maidstone examples were later acquired. The big change came in July 1979 when the first of many modern Daimler Fleetlines discarded by London Transport entered service. They were prepared by Stevensons and the centre-exit was usually removed in the process. Amongst the numerous examples placed into service was 31 (CBF 31Y) which we see in Uttoxeter bus station on 8 June 1984

carrying the revised livery. This bus was a curious rebuild of former London MCW-bodied Fleetline THM 689M of 1974, and used various parts from three other similar vehicles. The bus had been acquired in 1983 and entered service with Stevenson's registered as a new vehicle CBF 31Y. A pair of new Bristol VRT double-deckers with coach seating arrived in 1980/81 and by 1985 the fleet stood at around seventy vehicles. Following deregulation services expanded to cover a much bigger area, while a large number of modern buses were purchased both new and used. In June 1994 the decision was taken to sell the business which by then stood at an impressive 270 vehicles. It duly passed to British Bus, part of the Cowie Group.

(John Jones)

**Classic half-cabs.** Located approximately ten miles to the north-east of Cambridge is the village of Burwell on the southern edge of the Fens. In 1922 the Mansfield family founded a filling station and cycle business and were soon operating buses as well from premises in the village. From the outset a regular stage service from Burwell to Cambridge was operated, and soon other services were introduced, but of a much less frequent nature. These included one to Isleham and another from Soham to Bury St. Edmunds. Daimlers were a popular choice for this fleet from 1929 with many being purchased new including some interesting coaches. Double-deckers first appeared during WWII and some new examples appeared early on. EER 102 was a Daimler CWA6 with a Brush utility body while HER 784 was a 56-seat Massey-bodied Daimler CVD6

dating from January 1950. It is seen in Drummer Street bus station, Cambridge, in July 1968, and was followed into service in 1951 by similar vehicle JVE 447 which had a low-bridge body. Burwell and District later went on to buy an early Fleetline model, 9 DER, which was the first rear-engine double-decker in the Cambridge area. A second Fleetline was purchased, but subsequently many used double-deckers were acquired including AECs and latterly second-hand Fleetlines from City of Nottingham. Burwell and District ceased to trade on 9 June 1979, when they sold out to Eastern Counties. At this time they were still using the original site in High Street, Burwell, as their bus garage and filling station.

*(Cliff Essex collection)*

D Coaches was one of a number of independents in the Swansea area during the 1970s that ran luxury coaches but was also engaged in the provision of school transport. For contract work D Coaches operated a fleet of elderly double-deckers and saloons mostly of Bristol manufacture. Upon gaining a significant number of new contracts the school bus fleet rapidly expanded, and a fleet of thirty-two elderly Metro-Cammell bodied Leyland PD2s was acquired from Lothian Regional Transport in 1975/76. The livery also changed from light grey and orange band to white with black and orange stripes, although the Lothian Leylands were never repainted. D Coaches ran five Bristol Lodekkas,

four of which were of the LD5G variety as depicted here by VVF 203 and UNG 178, seen in the Llansamlet yard on 1 November 1975. Both were new to Eastern Counties with UNG joining the fleet from Smith of Garnswllt in May 1974, while VVF arrived via Newton, Dingwall in September 1975. A former City of Oxford AEC Bridgemaster was by now perhaps the odd-man-out in a fleet of Bristol and Leyland double-deckers and did not stay long. D Coaches remained involved with school contracts in the Swansea area until January 2011, when the business closed down.

*(Andrew Wiltshire)*

Lancashire United Transport (LUT) was for many years one of Britain's largest independent bus operators, and operated a large number of double-deckers. They were founded in 1925 as Lancashire United Tramways to acquire the assets of the failing South Lancashire Electric Traction and Power Co, and were based at Atherton near Leigh west of Manchester. The first double-deckers arrived in 1925 and by 1927 were operating numerous services. The Guy Arab was the preferred choice of chassis after WWI. Lancashire United were one of the very first customers for the Guy Arab IV model, taking a batch of ten in late 1951 numbered 452-61 (MTJ 91-100). They had 57-seat Weymann bodies, featured new-look bonnets and introduced a simple all-over red livery with one cream band. 459 is seen here very late on in its life at Bolton on 31 May 1966, in company with Bolton Corporation vehicles. After fifteen years' service, 459 would be withdrawn later in 1966. From 1956 thirty-foot double-deckers became standard and in addition to Guy Arab IVs, interesting types continued to appear with Dennis Lolines, Leyland PD3s, Daimler CSG6-30s and a solitary Guy Wulfrunian added to stock.

*(Malcolm Keeley)*

Matthews Coaches was established in the 1920s as a family business based at Shouldham, a village in Norfolk south of King's Lynn. They operated a small number of double-deckers in the 1960s and 1970s and these included LYR 979, an ex-London Transport RT, YCY 805 a former South Wales Transport AEC Regent V and HNW 365D, a Leyland PD3A which was new to Farsley Omnibus Co. Of particular interest was a pair of Daimlers which they acquired from Chesterfield Corporation in December 1973. Chesterfield had previously bought front-engine Daimlers in 1955/56, but had more recently opted for Leyland PD2s. It was a little surprising when in December 1963 they bought ten Daimler CCG6 with Weymann 65-seat bodies and constant-mesh gearboxes, followed by a further eight in late 1965. They were not popular with drivers and the first examples were withdrawn as early as 1972. Most went for further service and several ended up in Hong Kong being converted to semi-automatic configuration. Matthews bought 3257/9 NU and here we see the latter in as-acquired condition in July 1974. It did later receive blue and white fleet livery and was withdrawn in 1978, whereas 3257 NU had been sold by May 1976. Matthews of Shouldham continue to operate a thriving coaching business to this day, although it is many years since they operated double-deckers.

*(Andrew Wiltshire collection)*

On 4 July 1973 at Penzance we find this twenty five year old former Plymouth Corporation Leyland PD2/1, belonging to Harvey's Blue and Cream Bus Service. DJY 945 has a Leyland 53-seat body and formed part of a batch of sixty five similar buses delivered in 1948/49, Plymouth's first Leyland PD2s and also their last low-bridge type buses. DJY 945 had been acquired in 1966 to replace a former Plymouth Leyland PD1, and joined DJY 959 which had been with Harvey since 1963. N R Harvey and Sons was a very small operator based in Mousehole near Penzance and their primary role was the shared operation of the service from Penzance to Newlyn and Mousehole. This was originally shared with Western National and Hitchens of Newlyn, until the latter sold out to Western National in 1966. The nature of this route required small buses due to narrow streets in Newlyn and Mousehole and in the early 1960s Harvey was using a pair of Bedford OBs, joined in 1966 by an ex Halifax Albion Nimbus. The double-deckers were used mainly for contract work including schools services, and DJY 959 was replaced by an ex Sheffield Atlantean in 1973. DJY 945 however, soldiered on until eventually being sold for preservation in 1982. Finally two Bristol LHS saloons were acquired new in 1977 and 1981 for the stage service, which eventually passed to Western National in 1988, and Harvey's went out of business.

(Malcolm Keeley)

Berresfords Motors Ltd was a well-known family run independent operator and its demise has been mourned by many. Initially Harold Berresford based at Ubberley Farm began running in 1919, a Ford Model T from nearby Bucknall to Hanley. By 1923 James Berresford was operating a Hanley to Leek service from Wetley Rocks and larger vehicles were gradually introduced. From 1924 this route was shared with PMT and Procter while in 1930 a Leek to Longton service was established. The family acquired a large site at Cheddleton in 1935 and this became their new base while a limited company was formed in 1938. During WWII the fleet of Berresfords Motors Ltd grew with new works contracts and the first double-deckers arrived in 1950. The policy of Jim Berresford was to obtain good quality used buses, and a variety of AEC Regents, Leyland Titans were to grace the fleet for many years. KEK 745 is one of a number of former Wigan Leyland PD2A/27 models in the fleet during the 1970s. It has a Northern Counties body and dates from 1963. It has been parked on the forecourt of the Cheddleton premises, having just brought the author from Longton on 30 March 1978. Batches of buses were often purchased and some would only be used for spares, but most would end their days dumped in Berresfords legendary "bus graveyard" at Cheddleton. Following the death of Jim Berresford, Berresfords Motors Ltd sold out to former NBC subsidiary PMT on 16 May 1987.

*(Andrew Wiltshire)*

Bagillt is a small North Wales town between Flint and Shotton which were centres of industry in the last century. Price and Owen Lloyd founded their business in Bagillt in 1926 and were soon gainfully employed on works contracts to the nearby Shotton Steelworks complex, Courtauld's two factories at Flint and a third at Greenfield; and also some colliery services. Between 1949 and 1959, four new double-deckers were purchased, all with Massey bodies. In 1949 Lloyd's took a Foden PVD6 which was followed in October 1955 by a 62-seat Guy Arab IV. A further Arab IV was added to the fleet, but this time a thirty foot model. This is the subject of our photograph taken at Bagillt on 14 July 1975. RDM 200 a 73-seater was new in May 1958 and served Lloyd's for over twenty years, latterly used on school services. It was eventually sold for preservation and spent a number of years stored near Ormskirk until exported to Germany in 1997. The final new addition was a Leyland PD3 SDM 663 in March 1959. From then on it was second-hand double-deckers as school contracts increased, and the works contracts ceased as local industries closed down. All wore Lloyd's smart cream livery with red bands, and were based at Rhydwen Garage in Bagillt.

*(John Jones)*

Whittlesey is a small town in Cambridgeshire on the eastern edge of Peterborough. Independent operator T Canham and Sons (Services) Ltd founded in 1922 was based in the town and ran a service from Whittlesey into Peterborough. During the 1950s they had DLU 40, an ex-London Transport STL AEC Regent, which they used on the Peterborough service until 1959. In May 1971 the firm of Bluebell Buses of March was acquired, which included two vehicles, together with their daily March to Wisbech route and the March town service. Between March 1971 and May 1972 a trio of 1953-vintage ECW low-bridge Bristol KSW5Gs were purchased from Eastern National. They were VNO 863/5/6 and VNO 863 is seen here at Bishopsgate old bus station, Peterborough, in June 1971. The two former Bluebell Buses services passed to J W Embling & Sons of Guyhirn in June 1977, while the last two double-deckers owned were EOO 589 and 828 SHW, a pair of Bristol FLF6Bs which arrived in 1977 and 1979 respectively. Canham's used a blue and cream livery for many years, but changed to orange and cream in about 1981, while in October 1983 they suddenly ceased trading after 61 years.

*(Cliff Essex)*

The Whippet business was founded in 1919 by Mr H Lee using a Ford Model T that had been converted into a bus. Initially based in the Cambridgeshire village of Graveley, its premises were located at nearby Hilton by 1935. The Whippet name was introduced early on, and services to Cambridge, St Ives and St Neots were soon undertaken. A limited company Whippet Coaches Ltd was formed in 1935 and by 1938 the fleet included a Chevrolet, several Gilfords, Bedfords and Dennis. Leylands later appeared and in 1949 a number of Crossley coaches were purchased new. As business grew there became a need for larger buses and the first double-decker, a former Huddersfield Daimler arrived in 1955.

Double-deckers were then regularly purchased and Whippet ran a variety of types including Guy Arabs, AEC Regent IIIs and Vs as well as Leyland PD2s and PD3s. This AEC Bridgemaster came from Ronsway of Hemel Hempstead in 1970, and was one of a pair new to Scottish independent Smith of Barrhead in 1961. Seen at the depot in October 1970, 29 EGD was the only forward-entrance front-engine double-decker ever acquired by Whippet, but a rear-entrance Bridgemaster was obtained in 1973. Both were sold in 1976. Further double-deck additions would be mainly Leyland manufacture when used Atlanteans started to appear from 1978.

*(Cliff Essex)*

Wade Emmerson began operating buses as early as 1912, in the Evenwood area of County Durham. In 1928 he entered into a joint venture with a Mr Howe from Spennymoor and a Mr Blenkinsop of West Cornforth, to operate a service from Bishop Auckland to Newcastle upon Tyne. At this point the name OK Motor Services was adopted. AEC and Leyland saloons formed the mainstay of the fleet until 1946 when the first double-deckers arrived. Many former London Transport Leylands of both RTL and RTW variety were added to stock in the 1950s, while in 1958 a new Leyland PD3 was obtained. AEC Regent Vs would eventually be found running alongside a wide variety of second hand Leyland PD2 and PD3 models, and OK went on to acquire a small fleet of early

Atlanteans when they came on to the market. WVH 420 dating from 1963, was one of three Roe-bodied Leyland PD3A/2s that came from West Yorkshire PTE in 1976, having been new to Huddersfield Corporation Transport. It is seen entering the Market Place at Bishop Auckland on 8 June 1978. From 1973 a number of new Leyland Atlanteans were purchased followed by a solitary Dennis Dominator, and then six smart Leyland Olympians. OK prospered greatly after deregulation in 1986, growing rapidly in size, but alas was feeling the effects of increasing competition by 1994. The business passed to the Go Ahead Group in March 1995, by which time it had 212 vehicles based on five sites.

*(John Jones)*

Southern Vectis received their first batch of Bristol LD6Gs between March and May 1954. They were given fleet numbers 500-21 and were initially allocated to rail replacement services, being fitted with large luggage racks over both rear wheel-arches, which explains the original seating capacity of H33/21R. They lost the nearside luggage rack in 1957, and the offside by 1964, giving them 27 seats in the lower saloon. They were gradually withdrawn from 1969 onwards with the last examples coming off in 1975. 505 (KDL 401) was withdrawn in September 1971 and passed to Worcestershire independent Jones Brothers of Great Malvern by May 1972. Here it joined ex City of Oxford AEC Regent III UWL 931, and former South Wales Transport AEC Regent V NCY 458, which Jones had acquired in early 1967. In this view taken on 17 June 1973, we see KDL 401 in "as-acquired" condition, and it is thought that its main duty was on a school contract to Upton on Severn. For many years Jones had also operated a coach fleet. KDL 401 was withdrawn in October 1976 and was later cut-down for use as a towing wagon, being scrapped at some point after 1981.

*(John Jones)*

Based in the village of Bures in Suffolk, the business of H C Chambers can be traced back as far as 1877 when a stable and saddlery operation began running horse-drawn buses, and inaugurated a service from Sudbury to Colchester. Motor buses were introduced from 1918 and the service was subsequently extended northwards to Bury St Edmunds. The onset of WWII saw services expand and loadings increase. Double-deckers were required, and both new and second-hand and Guy Arabs proved to be a very popular choice, with the last new example, an Arab IV, arriving in 1957. Ten years later in May 1967 the first of three Guy Arab IIIs with low-bridge Duple bodywork, HWO 341, was obtained from Red and White. This was followed by HWO 339 in November and HWO 333 in March 1969. In this view we see HWO 339 at Colchester in June 1969. All three of these fine-looking buses were sold for scrap in 1972, while Chambers switched to running modern lightweight saloons for the rest of the 1970s and most of the following decade. A return to double-deck operation began from 1989 and twenty years later a big fleet of Leyland Olympians, mostly second-hand, was in use. On 28 May 2012, H C Chambers and Sons Ltd sold out to the Go Ahead group, and in 2015 it retains its identity, but operates out of the Hedingham (Go Ahead) depot at Sudbury.

*(Cliff Essex)*

Continental Pioneer Ltd was formed in 1964 by Tim Lewis, and a number of former British European Airways (BEA) one and a half-deck AEC Regal coaches were acquired for use on a programme of European camping tours, an activity which had ceased by 1978. Meanwhile, back in 1966 industrial action by some London Transport platform staff led to LT having to withdraw a small number of services which were immediately taken on by independent operators. Isleworth coaches operated the 235 from Richmond Town Centre to Richmond Hill until May 1968 when it passed to Continental Pioneer who ran it until September 1980. This was normally the preserve of saloons but occasionally double-deckers like LLU 829 were called upon to perform. Formerly London Transport RTL1050, a 1950 vintage Leyland 7RT with a Park Royal body it was used in a movie before sale to Continental Pioneer. After passing to Ted Brakell, a bus dealer based in Cheam, it lost its roof for use as a promotional vehicle. Happily, it later regained a roof from a scrapped RT and ultimately passed into preservation.

*(Andrew Wiltshire collection)*

Gash of Newark received nine new Daimler CVD6 double-deckers between 1948 and 1951. Following on from DD1 to DD4 (described on page 3) they took delivery of DD5/6 (KNN 958/9) with Roberts 56-seat high-bridge bodywork which were later fitted with platform doors. DD5 survived until 1969, while DD6 was ultimately preserved after withdrawal in 1978. The last Daimler CVD6s were DD7 to DD9 with Duple low-bridge bodywork, and were delivered new with platform doors. DD7/8 (LNN 353, LRR 403) were actually ordered by Skill of Nottingham and were to have been registered LTO 20/30, while DD9 (MRR 8) was ordered by Oxfordshire-based Heyfordian. DD8 is seen here at the Bowbridge Road garage in August 1976. All three survived with Gash until the late 1970s, with DD7/8 entering preservation. Gash took a tenth Daimler in 1954, a CVG6 model with new-look bonnet and Massey body, after which no double-deckers were purchased until 1979, when a smart new Leyland Atlantean joined the fleet. From 1969 Leyland Leopard saloons formed the mainstay of the service bus fleet with double-deckers only appearing on the Nottingham service at busy times. This all changed after deregulation in 1986 when Gash took on many new routes and purchased an interesting selection of used double-deckers. Sadly, W Gash and Sons Ltd sold out to Lincolnshire Road Car Co in May 1989.

*(the late Les Ring)*

In addition to their service bus fleet, A.A. Motor Services member Dodds of Troon operated a modern coach fleet and also kept two preserved vehicles. One of these was SJW 515, a rare Guy Warrior LUF with a Burlingham Seagull coach body that, as a Guy demonstrator, had been new with a Meadows engine. It was later fitted with an AEC AH470 engine by Dodds. The other preserved vehicle was OKM 317, the well-known AEC Regent III 9612E that was built in June 1949, for use as a demonstrator by Saunders, Beaumaris, builder of its 56-seat lightweight body. It was eventually registered in December 1951 when it went on loan to Maidstone and District. The following year it passed to A.A. Motor Services member Charles Law of Prestwick, who ran it until he left the cooperative in November 1953. Law's vehicles were then shared among the remaining A.A. members Dodds, Tumilty and Young. OKM 317 became Dodds fleet number D.T. No.13, and remained an active part of this fleet until July 1979. It is seen at Troon as a preserved bus during a PSV Circle AGM visit on 31 March 1985. It is now thought to be preserved at the Beith Transport Museum.

*(John Jones)*

Samuel Eynon, a former miner at Trimsaran Colliery, purchased a Leyland in about 1921/22 and began operating it between Trimsaran and Llanelli. The route was extended to Carmarthen in 1926, and by the mid-1930s Eynon was running a number of services in the area. The first double-decker was an ex Red and White Leyland TD2, acquired in 1948 while in 1950, a pair of brand new all-Leyland PD2s arrived. Leyland was always the preferred but not exclusive choice for double-deckers, and the front-engined PD2 and PD3 models were purchased right up to the early 1980s, even after a brief flirtation with Atlanteans. On 21 March 1984, we are in the village of Trimsaran for this view of FEK 1F working to Llanelli, although the destination blind misleadingly says Kidwelly. Acquired in 1981, it is a Leyland PD2/37 with Massey 64-seat forward-entrance bodywork that had previously worked for Greater Manchester PTE as their 3290. It had been new to Wigan Corporation (25) in 1968, one of a batch of nine and the last half-cabs for that undertaking. FEK 1F passed to Davies, Pencader, in 1988 with the Eynon business and was withdrawn in July 1990. As a withdrawn bus it was re-registered ODE 47F and sold for preservation in 1992.

*(John Wiltshire)*

D.J. Watkins (Prestatyn Coachways), Meliden commenced operations in 1955 with a Leyland TS7. The first double-decker to appear was a former Crosville Bristol K6A that Watkins obtained from Owen of Holyhead in September 1969. This was replaced during 1971 by a pair of rare Daimler CSG6-30s from Lancashire United. Watkins also ran a number of coaches and by the early 1970s had adopted the Prestatyn Coachways fleetname, whilst continuing to purchase an interesting variety of double-deckers for use on school contracts. These included a former Stratford Blue Leyland PD2, a pair of Bristol LDs and also in 1976, a pair of forward-entrance Dennis Lolines from Alder Valley. From December 1981 the legal entity of the fleet changed to Prestatyn Coachways by which time a pair of Leyland PD2/40s with Metro-Cammell bodywork, WRJ 182/4, had arrived from Blythin (Gold Star) of St. Asaph. These buses had been new to Salford City Transport in 1963 and WRJ 184 is noted at Prestatyn Coachways premises at Gwaenysgor Road, Dyserth on 30 August 1982. A number of rear-engined double-deckers, mainly Daimler Fleetlines and Leyland Atlanteans were also owned over the years, but the numbers dwindled and by 2000 only one was recorded. It is believed that Prestatyn Coachways went out of business around 2003.

*(John Jones)*

**Rear-engine Daimlers**. By early 1923 Jack Dean and Arthur Allen were running a bus service, based initially at Littleover near Derby. The service, which required three vehicles, linked Derby to Burton-upon-Trent via Repton and Willington, where route passed beneath a low bridge. Percy Tailby joined the business in 1924, followed by Harold George and the name Blue Bus Services was in use by 1926. From 1927 Tailby and George were the only remaining partners, and a new depot in Willington was opened in 1930. More services were started and the first double-deckers, four low-bridge Daimler CWA6s, were introduced during the war. The bridge at Willington precluded the use of normal-height double-deckers. Post-war, further Daimlers were purchased including CVG6s and four rare CD650 models which received low-bridge Willowbrook bodies. A pair of Dennis Lolines were acquired in 1957/58, which offered a low-height solution to the awkward sunken gangway layout. A pair of Daimler Fleetlines with low-height Northern Counties bodies arrived in 1962 with another in 1964. A fourth similar vehicle was JRB 481D which was new in 1966 and is seen here at Derby on 10 August 1973. The well-known prototype Fleetline 7000 HP was also purchased in 1966, while the final double decker, an Alexander-bodied Fleetline, arrived in 1971. Blue Bus Services sold out to Derby Corporation Transport on 1 December 1973, who chose to retain the Willington premises. Tragically, on the night of 5 January 1976, the entire garage at Willington and most of the former Blue Bus fleet was destroyed by fire.

*(John Wiltshire)*

Seaton Delaval is a large village in Northumberland between the seaside resort of Whitley Bay and the former mining town of Cramlington. In May 1927 a licence was granted to H W Hunter to run a service between Seaton Delaval and Whitley Bay and operations commenced in 1929. By 1931 it was also serving North Shields and did not change until 1977 when Hunter was granted permission to run into Cramlington. Double-deckers were eventually introduced in 1948 and in 1950/51 a pair of new all-Leyland PD2s arrived and served Hunter for over twenty years. The third and final new double-decker was a Leyland Atlantean in 1971, which did not last as long as the PD2s. At around this time Hunter changed hands and became H W Hunter and Sons (Seaton Delaval) Ltd and remained based at Westbourne Garage in the village. An interesting selection of used double-deckers passed through the fleet over the years. These included a pair of ex Leicester AEC Renowns, numerous former Newcastle and Tyne and Wear PTE Atlanteans and this Daimler Fleetline 45 (JHA 81E) with an Alexander body, that had been new in July 1967 as Midland Red 6081. It is seen here at Hunter's garage on 27 May 1979, having just been acquired, though it had been stripped for spares by March 1981. After deregulation the fleet expanded and their service was extended and given route number 810.

*(John Jones)*

Following the delivery of a Daimler Fleetline in 1963 (see page 35), this became the standard double-decker for McGill's Bus Service for the next ten years. All later deliveries however had Alexander bodies commencing with AHS 16B a 78-seater in 1964. The 1970 deliveries had panoramic windows and dual-door layout, which proved unsatisfactory and were later rebuilt to single-door with normal-size windows on the lower deck. The last four Fleetlines arrived between 1971 and 1973 and had low-height single-door bodies, and surprisingly they were to be the first ones sold, all having left the fleet by 1980. Seen in Paisley on 29 May 1978 is CHS 721C, one of a trio new in 1965. McGill's had a complete change of vehicle policy from 1976 when it took delivery of a new pair of 52-seat Leyland National single-deckers. Six further Leyland Nationals were acquired new, followed by eight of the revised Leyland National 2 model. A pair of Leyland-DAB articulated buses was trialled between 1984 and 1987 on an express service into the centre Glasgow, just as double-deck operations were coming to an end. McGill's Bus Service Ltd sold out to Clydeside 2000 in July 1997, by which time Dennis Dart and DAF saloons were being operated alongside the remaining Leyland Nationals.

*(John Jones)*

Hartas Foxton was running Red Bus Service of York shortly after the end of the First World War and in 1926 formed an agreement with Norman Pearce (Pullman of York) to share the York to Stamford Bridge service. In 1929 he bought out the Pullman business, and integrating it with his Red Bus Service, he created the York Pullman Bus Company. Other operators were acquired in subsequent years which introduced coaches to the fleet, and Dennis was a popular choice of chassis. York Pullman was based at offices in the 13th century Bootham Tower in Exhibition Square in York, and kept its vehicles in a purpose-built garage in Navigation Road which was erected in 1938. The first double-deckers, a trio of Regent IIIs with Roe bodies, arrived in 1954 reflecting a move to AEC chassis. A fourth example arrived in 1955 followed by Regent Vs in 1957 and 1964. Roe bodywork continued to be favoured for fitting to four Daimler Fleetlines, the first of which arrived in 1971. 107 (FDN 583S) was the final example new in November 1977 and, unlike the first three, featured peaked roof domes. It is seen turning into Exhibition Square on 24 March 1979. Double-deck operation ended in 1985 when York Pullman was taken over by Reynard's Rent-a-car of York, and the four remaining services were left in the hands of saloons. All traces of the original business had gone by 2000, but in 2007, K & J Logistics revived the York Pullman name and introduced some local services which they held until 2012.

*(John Jones)*

S Turner and Sons Ltd hailed from Brown Edge in Staffordshire and was one of many small independent fleets running in this area. Samuel Turner started running a 14-seat Ford Model T from Brown Edge into Hanley in 1920, a distance of some five miles. The route became licensed in 1922. Early vehicles included a number of Leyland saloons usually purchased new and the first double-deckers were Leyland TD4s and an AEC Regent, all ex-Salford, in 1951. Further used Leyland Titans entered the fleet in the years up to 1955, while a pair of RT-type AEC Regents had arrived from London Transport by 1958. Double-deckers usually outnumbered the small coach fleet, a 1957 Massey-bodied Leyland PD2 being the first bought new. Massey continued to be favoured for a pair of forward-entrance PD3s in 1959 and 1962, while the last half-cab for Turners was a 64-seat PD2 in 1964. They then turned to rear-engined buses, receiving eight new Northern Counties bodied Fleetlines, plus a used pair from London Transport. The last new one, badged as a Leyland, was 8 (LVT 699V) delivered in April 1980, and seen here at the Brown Edge depot on 8 December 1980. Turners retained conductor operation to the end, which came in 1988 when they were taken over by former NBC subsidiary PMT.

*(Andrew Wiltshire)*

In 1968 Daimler persuaded Ronald Edgley Cox, the General Manager of Walsall Corporation Transport, to try out one of its huge CRC6-36 chassis. Cox, with a reputation as an innovator, was keen to assist Daimler who had secured an order from South Africa. The Walsall bus 56 (XDH 56G) was exhibited at the 1968 Commercial Motor Show and attracted much attention. It had a Cummins V6-200 9.63-litre engine of 150bhp, mounted in the rear offside corner of the chassis and had a fully-automatic gearbox and power steering. Its Northern Counties body was plain but impressive. Its overall length of 36ft provided 86 seats, despite having a second staircase and door at the extreme rear. It was intended as a driver-only bus, and featured a CCTV system to monitor the rear exit, as well as an electronic passenger counter for upper saloon. In reality, it only ever ran with a conductor and was later converted to semi-automatic transmission. After passing to the West Midlands PTE in 1969, the bus saw sporadic use until withdrawal in 1975. It passed to Vale of Llangollen Tours (Roberts) of Cefn Mawr in May 1976, who kept it for less than a year. Its final owner was Lea Valley (Hale Brothers Coaches) of Bishops Stortford from July 1978, as seen in this view; and whose persistence and enthusiasm ensured it ran until 1986. It was subsequently rescued for preservation, and now resides at the Transport Museum, Wythall, where it has been restored to full working order in its original sky blue and cream livery.

*(Andrew Wiltshire collection)*

The Primrose Valley Garage and Coach Co, of Filey, was founded in 1951 with the acquisition of a Bedford OB. It was based at premises in Primrose Valley Road and for many years operated a predominantly Bedford coach fleet. Its proprietors were A Webster and A Elley and in addition to extensive excursion and private hire work, two seasonal stage services were operated, serving the holiday camps in the area. For this, second-hand heavyweight saloons were generally purchased, often AEC Reliances, interesting exceptions being 862 RAE a former Bristol Omnibus Bristol SUS, and also NAH 661F, a rare Bedford VAM/ECW, new to Eastern Counties. The first double-decker arrived in 1976 in the form of ex City of Nottingham Daimler Fleetline 78 RTO, an early example dating from 1963 and fitted with Northern Counties 79-seat body, and which would no doubt be a useful machine in the summer season. It was often used on a run from Reighton Sands Holiday Park to Dennis's Holiday Park, but is thought to have been sold in 1979. It is seen at Filey Camp in July 1978. In the years after deregulation in 1986, the stage services were extended and could now be found running into both Scarborough and Bridlington and once again double-deckers were employed. These tended to be former Greater Manchester PTE Leyland Atlanteans, and Fleetlines from West Midlands PTE, which included at least one former London Transport DMS.

*(Cliff Essex)*

A1 Service NCS 11P was a 1976 Daimler Fleetline with an Alexander 74-seat body and is seen in Ardrossan on 28 May 1978. It was one of a trio new to Murray of Saltcoats that year, while seven other similar buses were delivered to other members. Murray also ran three earlier Alexander-bodied Fleetlines, and went on to buy his last new one in 1979. By 1980 the number of A1 members had increased to fifteen, with the split of the Hunter, Crosshouse, fleet. J Hunter then set up in his own membership in Kilmarnock using Atlanteans and a pair of unusual Van Hool-bodied Ailsas. Volvo had introduced the front-engine Ailsa double-deck chassis in 1973, which was actually built at a Volvo plant in Irvine on A1's main route. It came as no surprise when A1 members purchased three new examples in 1976 followed by a further eight up to 1979. Other new types of double-decker introduced to the A1 operation were the Volvo Citybus, Scania, and inevitably the Leyland Olympian. After deregulation in 1986, members were often attracted to relatively modern used double-deckers while the use of saloons increased very slightly. The Ayrshire Bus Owners cooperative continued until January 1995 when it passed to the Stagecoach Group. The A1 Service brand was however retained as a fleet-name on the buses in the former A1 territory until 2010.

*(John Jones)*

**Special duties.** During the 1980s and even into the 1990s, front-engine double-deckers with manual transmission were still very much sought after, but rarely for passenger-carrying duties. A number of larger fleets, many of whom had long since disposed of such types were buying up one or two for driver-training duties. In addition to this, smaller firms, often driving schools would be looking to acquire manual gearbox AEC Regent Vs or Leyland Titans (PD2 or PD3) to use as a training buses. Much of this came about in the wake of deregulation, when there was an increased demand for new drivers with a full PSV licence, to drive manual gearbox minibuses. For this role Trevor Thomas of Williamstown

near Penygraig in the Rhondda purchased a Taff-Ely AEC Regent V in April 1983, but only kept it until September. He replaced it with GRY 54D, a 1966 Leyland PD3A/1 with a Metro-Cammell body, which had previously been with Hollis of Queensferry, but had been new to Leicester City Transport. GRY 54D is captured in action at Tonypandy on 19 April 1986, with the photographer's younger brother in the driving seat! The bus was eventually sold in January 1988 to Davies of Carmarthen, who subsequently sold it to Southend Transport as a trainer in 1990.

*(John Jones)*

Particularly common in industrial and mining communities like South Wales, dance troupes and marching jazz bands would regularly take part in competitions. Many groups found it made sense to own their own dedicated transport, usually an old bus or coach. One such vehicle was Roe-bodied Leyland Atlantean JRH 417E, which was used by the Woodmansey Beavers Junior Jazz Band who were based in the Yorkshire village of that name, to the south east of Beverley. The bus is seen at Beverley on 16 September 1986 having started life with Kingston-upon-Hull Corporation Transport (217) in January 1967, after withdrawal by them in June 1986. Hull was a big user of double-deckers and also a keen Atlantean operator, having received their first examples in 1960. This particular vehicle was one of a batch of fifteen, and featured the unusual one-piece flat windscreen that was favoured by Hull at this time. It had passed from the Beavers to a jazz band in Doncaster by 1991, and was in preservation the following year. However it then passed to a dealer by 2001 and may well have been exported in 2003. Similar bus JRH 214E is currently preserved in Hull.

*(John Jones)*

Halls Coaches Ltd of Hounslow who traded as Silverline Tours, started airport transfer services at Heathrow using former London Transport RFs. In 1969 they secured a contract with American-owned TWA (Trans World Airlines) to provide transfers from central London to Heathrow Terminal 3, and for this they acquired VYH 46-8G, three new Leyland Atlantean PDR2/1 models with 68-seat Roe bodies featuring a luggage compartment in the lower saloon. In April 1972 a further five long-wheelbase Atlanteans were delivered, again with Roe bodies, but to Leeds City Transport, and were registered LLH 5-9K. In August 1973 the eighty-five strong fleet of Halls of Hounslow (Silverline Tours Ltd) passed to Tricentrol Ltd of Dunstable which then gave the Tricentrol Travel Group a fleet of 149. The use of the double-deckers on airport transfer work soon came to an end and the eight Atlanteans were sold off, all of them being eagerly snapped up by independent operators. LLH 9K, the subject of our photograph is seen in London while working for Halls. It passed to Cottrell of Mitcheldean in 1974 where a destination box was fitted for the first time and the luggage compartment was removed. Here it put in a further fifteen years' service before becoming a mobile shop in Northampton.

*(John Wiltshire collection)*

Heading further west into South Wales we now come across a double-decker in use as a promotional vehicle for a car dealership, posed in a pleasant sunny location on 19 April 1981. In 1950 T B Gravell began operating PSVs, and around 1963 started trading as Pinged Hill Garage, Pinged Hill being a small village near Kidwelly. Never a large fleet, from 1959 it consisted of a single vehicle and, until 1971, this was one of three new bus-bodied Bedford SBs operated in succession for use on a colliery contract. A new SB coach followed, which was replaced in 1975 by a Bedford YRQ coach, from Corvedale of Ludlow. When PSV operations ceased in April 1976, the YRQ passed, along with their licence, to Eynon's of Trimsaran. Gravell's were also a Renault car and minibus dealership with several premises, and it is at their showroom on the Gwaun-cae-Gurwen road out of Ammanford that we see 430 HCY. It is an AEC Regent V with a Park Royal body that was new to South Wales Transport. The bus had been prepared for its role with Gravell's by none other than Eynon's of Trimsaran, during the summer of 1980. It remained a promotional vehicle until November 1983, and had passed to a Barnsley breaker by May 1984.

*(John Jones)*

Lesley Smith and Rodney Smith (unrelated) established an industrial die-casting factory in Hackney, east London, in 1947. Lesney Products & Co. Ltd went on to develop a small die-cast toy that could fit into a matchbox which proved to be an instant hit, and so Matchbox Toys came into being. Lesney required a fleet of buses to transport its workers to and from the site in Hackney, and over the years a large variety of vehicles appeared. The transport fleet was originally provided and maintained by PVS Sales which was associated with Super Coaches of Upminster, and later City Coach Lines, and vehicles often moved between the fleet and Lesney. Since 1972 this service was provided by Ensign of Hornchurch, a bus dealer who initially supplied, amongst other buses, Leyland PD2s from Leeds and Midland Red, Bristol Ks and Lodekkas from Tilling Group companies, as well as a large number of former London RTs. One slightly more unusual vehicle was LKG 664, an AEC Regent V with a low-bridge Park Royal 59-seat body that had been new to Western Welsh in March 1956. In June 1972 the bus passed to Gelligaer Urban District Council where it was used on service and for driver training. In March 1974 it passed to Ensign, and it is seen here on 7 August 1975 at work on a Lesney contract. LKG 664 was sold for scrap in May 1976.

*(Andrew Wiltshire collection)*

Herbert Hill Brain, was born in 1864 in Kingswood, Bristol. He founded a grocery business locally in 1890, and in 1927 began producing meat products on a site in Upper York Street. Mr Brain's Faggots were introduced and were later made in the Brains (Food Products) Ltd factory at Bridge Road in Kingswood, and for many years they ran a fleet of elderly buses for staff transport. During the 1970s five former Bristol Omnibus Company double-deckers were a familiar sight around the eastern suburbs of Bristol, including PHW 966 which is seen at the factory on 20 February 1976. It was an ECW-bodied Bristol KSW6B dating from 1953 that had been purchased in 1969, and ran until 1981 when it was exported to France. A similar bus in use was NHY 994, which also lasted with Brains until 1981. Three 7ft 6in wide Bristol K6Bs were operated and comprised LHU 382, LHY 929 together with LAE 316, which retained Tilling green. The Brain's bus fleet was maintained "in house" and during 1976 the company was taken over by the American-based Kraft Foods. The staff bus operation continued until about 1981, by which time a pair of former Bristol Omnibus FLF-type Lodekkas had been added to the fleet. It is thought that the factory was eventually closed down in about 2003.

*(Andrew Wiltshire)*

The Hales business was started in Clevedon in 1926 by Frank Hale. By the mid-1930s the business was employing 200, and in 1938 a Swiss roll production line was opened. Part of the company was later sold to Fitch & Son, food wholesalers, who in 1962 merged Hales with the John Trent cake business of London to form Hales-Trent Cakes. The Clevedon factory with a workforce of approximately 900 was acquired in 1974 by Lyons Bakery Ltd. Staff transport was a major consideration for Hales-Trent and over the years a number of interesting buses were operated as non-PSVs. One of the earliest double-deckers recorded was VAM 944 (see front cover), one of the former Silver Star Leyland Atlanteans which was purchased from Berresfords of Cheddleton in 1969, whilst MCO 669 was an ex Plymouth City Transport Leyland PD2. In 1974 Hales-Trent bought a pair of new Bedford SB5 buses with bodywork by Strachan and these replaced two Bedford VAM5s also with Strachan bodies that had been new in 1966. A surprise purchase in March 1975 was HHT 57N, a brand new Leyland Atlantean AN68 with a 72-seat East Lancs bodywork, which we see at the Clevedon site on 29 May 1975. It had no destination box and was without power-steering. In 1987 the Hales-Trent factory at Clevedon was closed and demolished and the site is now home to offices. As for HHT 57N, it passed to Cedar Coaches of Bedford and was licensed as a PSV for the first time.

*(John Wiltshire)*